PRAISE FOR *POINTS OF ATTACK*

"These rich, epigrammatic essays cover the waterfront of contemporary life, culture, and the self, flashing with insight and making us think in ways that bring home how little we ordinarily do so. By turns inducing perplexity and strengthening conviction, they aim not to tear us down but to build us up. De Silva admirably models the wakeful, agile intelligence we need if we are to make it through the dark alleys of the future morally intact and sound of mind and body."

Jacob Howland, author of *Glaucon's Fate: History, Myth, and Character in Plato's* Republic

"A sexy philosopher's almanac, a comet tail of ideas and personal truths, *Points of Attack* is that rare tonic that will dazzle you with its intellectual spectrum, and all the attention it pays to our burning world."

Siddharth Dhanvant Shanghvi, author of *Loss*

"A brash, engaging set of salvos that complicate our personal and political conditions."

Kirkus Reviews

POINTS OF ATTACK

MARK DE SILVA

170
SILVA

15.95

ISBN: 978-1-944866-76-1

Copyright © Mark de Silva

Cover by Matthew Revert

matthewrevertdesign.com

CLASH Books

clashbooks.com

To venture an opinion is like moving a piece at chess: it may be taken, but it forms the beginning of a game that is won.

Johann Wolfgang von Goethe

Contents

Foreword

When asked to explain what it was about Bernard Hopkins, the oldest champion in the history of boxing, that set him apart in the ring, the former middleweight Robert Allen offered the following enigmatic assessment: "He's not really a fighter. It's like something more political when you get in there with him."

This remark puts me in mind of certain questions I have concerning Mark de Silva. What is it about him that sets him apart from other philosophers? Is he not really a philosopher? When you get in there with him, what exactly is it more like than philosophy?

Let's take each question in turn.

In the days when de Silva worked at the *New York Times,* he could be observed in the cafeteria at lunch, sitting in a corner by himself and staring meaningfully into space. He did not bring with him reading matter; he did not swipe away at the screen of his smartphone. His behavior was eccentric: he appeared to be . . . thinking.

About what? Who knows. Boxing, clowns, terrorism, the nature of rationality. What matters is that he was engaged in sustained, independent, critical reflection about things. His mind was not stuck in a written text. He was not dutifully following a cultural dispute or political issue or philosophical debate in the accepted terms in which it was being litigated in newspapers or magazines or scholarly publications. Something he had read or heard or seen suggested an idea to him, and he would develop that idea in ways that he found compelling.

What is it about de Silva that sets him apart from other philosophers? Perhaps that he sits alone and thinks.

Is de Silva not really a philosopher? Maybe not. He has a Ph.D. in philosophy from the University of Cambridge, but he left academia to think and write more freely. Does this make him less of a philosopher? More of one?

He ended up writing a novel called *Square Wave*, which I would encourage you to run out and buy because you won't be able to put it down, except that that's not the kind of book it is, or the kind of reader de Silva is looking to reach. He wants fiction that you must put down. Fiction that forces you to sit alone and think.

The job of the philosopher, Wittgenstein wrote, amounts to "assembling reminders for a particular purpose." What did he mean by that phrase? Something like: offering piecemeal insights in service of a more unified aim. To be fragmented without being fragmentary. For Wittgenstein, his reminders, his fragments, sought to undermine a traditional picture of what philosophy was and should be.

De Silva assembles his own fragments, his own points of attack, in pursuit of no less ambitious a goal: an understanding of our world-historical moment. Yet, like Wittgenstein, he seeks not just to understand but also to suggest a different conception of what understanding might look like. It's not a theory or a thesis. It's something harder to pin down.

When you get in there with him, what exactly is it more like than philosophy? Lace up your gloves and find out.

James Ryerson

Preface

The Renaissance, the French Revolution, the fin de siècle, World War II—there are times when bedrock notions about human life fracture. Questions that once seemed more or less settled, even hardly worth asking, whether of citizenship, technology, the self, or the future of the species, are suddenly wide open once more. Between the twenty-first-century technologies refashioning contemporary life and the populist political energies threatening democratic pluralism and its globalized economic order, it is hard to doubt that we are living through one of these liminal moments, fraught as it is with uncertainties of every stripe: intellectual, political, psychosocial, personal.

It is in the midst of this tectonic shear, I think, that we have the most to gain in revisiting our assumptions in the widest possible way, across all departments of life—not only our ideas of how things are, but of how we would like them to be, so that we might know what to defend and what to stand against when all that was solid begins to crumble. Cultivating this kind of ecumenically critical mindset can help us remold our world more wisely and, no small thing, protect us against the partisan designs of those who would enlist us, through "fake news" and other spurious appeals, in the construction of far less agreeable futures. It also provides an opportunity, always welcome, to consider anew those things we think we know but perhaps do not, at least not as well as we thought, and to raise explicitly the questions we have only so far dimly pondered:

What does authenticity come to in a virtual world?
How should we understand climate-change denial?
Can terrorism ever be effective?
Is there such a thing as a too-long life?
Where does the power of parables reside?
Which artworks lose luster over time?
And when does collecting become hoarding?

Questions of this kind seem far more pressing today than they did only a decade ago, and I suspect the answers we should now give to them have changed. At a time when reckless and manipulative reasoning abounds, and merely keeping our intellectual bearings has become so taxing, it seems time to make a fresh start on them.

There are some peculiarities of treatment here worth mentioning at the outset. While it is my doctoral training in philosophy, which runs from aesthetics and politics to mind and language, that imbues this book with an intellectual interest it might have otherwise lacked, I have not abided those academic lessons slavishly. For one, I have refrained from imposing theoretical unity on my reflections, so that I might address each matter in as open a manner as possible, without cutting answers to fit preconceived shapes (shapes that are now shifting anyway). I have also assumed almost no prior knowledge on the part of readers, and have kept away from jargon, not just for the sake of accessibility, though there is that, but to unburden my meditations of philosophical baggage and avoid falling into the intellectual ruts that specialized vocabularies and "expert" knowledge encourage—in other words, to ensure that the start is truly *fresh* and might take us away from overworked lines of thought.

Finally, I have selected topics without an overarching scheme in mind. Instead, I have let my meditations roam, and allowed them to be nourished by my half dozen years in journalism at the *New York Times* and by my work as a novelist, too. In this way, I have extended the scope of this book quite beyond matters implicated in any obvious sense by recent social changes, trusting that affinities might emerge and that certain subtle shifts in attitude or orientation might be registered, if only implicitly, by the way they manifest across a broad swath of apparently unrelated issues.

Tellingly, themes did surface, and I have used them to group the entries. Among the many topics treated here are fears, from the persistence of terrorism to the age-old uncanniness of clowns. Freedoms of all sorts come in for scrutiny: human rights and the way talk of them can be abused; the coercive force of a sound argument; and the varieties of contemporary taboo and of defiance, too. With the nature and borders of the public sphere looming large today, cities and states each earn a chapter. One of the longest sections is dedicated—appropriately enough, in a time of transformation—to what our future might be like, for work and play, gender and medicine, poetry and higher learning. Language proved an almost inevitable theme, for it and the concepts we express by its means are mutating at an extraordinary rate. Sports—its ethics and boundaries, its meaning, too—occupies a more slender chapter, while the notion of character, moral, psychological, and otherwise, gets a longer one. The arts are given a good going-over: What makes a famous novelist disappear from cultural memory, say? Money, like war, could not be avoided: the appropriate limits of personal wealth, and what honoring soldiers requires, are dealt with, among other matters, in these two chapters. Naturally, this book of ruminations could only conclude with a few thoughts on philosophy itself and the good life.

A widely cast net, without doubt. Yet it might be the most authentic way of coming to grips with our moment, a kind of random sampling of all its corners, an allover painting of the time. The results I would not know how to summarize. I doubt that they can be, as what I present here are not conclusions so much as gestures, directions, points of attack. Taken together, I hope these eighty-odd inquiries into matters of common concern may serve as a cache of maps, necessarily incomplete, for navigating our cascading present.

FEARS

The Clowning Kind

The terror clowns may induce in us is a commonplace, yet for all that it remains poorly grasped. They frighten us for physiognomic reasons, their simulation of derangement. The clown's manner—his implacable jollity most of all—disturbs us in the way inapt feelings usually do: laughter at a funeral, say, or tears at a party. The incongruity is of a higher order, though, so that what we confront seems less like a personality disorder and more a form of psychosis.

The trouble we have is not with the clown's appearance, then, but with what it purports to tell us about the psyche within: What sort of person would carry himself like *that*? The more seamlessly a man inhabits the persona, the greater our unease; the more half-hearted the act—we have all witnessed clowns merely going through the motions—the less likely we are to be visited by a sense of uncanniness. The clowning appears only a mask for the man then, and we come to see him not as insane but as tragic, reduced by circumstance to slapstick for what we can only imagine to be a pittance. It is only fitting that the crying clown remains that brightest beacon of pathos.

Dementia Versus Death

If you're young, you'll not fear dementia much, though presumably you'll still fear death. After all, it might take you at any moment, and by so many means—you risk not having the chance to experience those milestones a full life grants. Dementia is not nearly so random: it prefers the elderly, and it runs a predictable course.

If you're getting on in years, though, you've been through a lot; there are fewer novel experiences left for you, compared with your younger days. Nonexistence may not frighten you quite so much anymore. You've done it all (or most of it), and you're inevitably growing weaker. What's so bad about calling it quits?

As you enter life's winter, you'll naturally fear you might be among those dementia unsouls. You have every reason to fear this, the more so the older you become, and you've no real way of knowing whether you'll be among those it spares. Then again, suppose it does come for you. Might this scattering of all you've grasped be precisely the respite you've been needing, in these final years, from the tedium of a world now too well known?

Terror's Efficacy

It is said the killing of innocents must compromise a terrorist's aims; indiscriminate violence costs him the very political capital he seeks among potential allies. Yet might the damage done to his cause, unquestionable though it is, be offset by greater gains? Might we even misunderstand his true aim altogether, so that what seems to us self-stultifying is, in truth, perfectly prudent?

To fix ideas, you could start with September 11, but April 19 will do just as well—the day in 1995 when libertarian terrorists gave their most unabashed American performance, in Oklahoma City. Can one seriously doubt, in either case, that unpleasant normative tensions that had felt faint and distant, tucked safely away in the corners of consciousness, came incandescently alive?

Since the Alfred P. Murrah building dematerialized and the Twin Towers lost their footing, I have—we have—found ourselves on newly intimate terms with Islamists and nationalist libertarians: with their rage first, yes, but later, and more lastingly, with their tortuous dream life. Would they not have remained strangers to us, had they declined to pain us so obscenely? Their brutality against the unsuspecting, and the turbidity of mind this has induced in us ever since, have given twenty-first-century American politics its shape. Even when we can't take seriously the radical spin, Islamism centripetally propels our government's intercourse abroad toward the center of our consciousness; just as domestic militia groups, not infrequently shading into Tea Party populists and white nationalists, exert this same curious force upon our government's behavior at home.

Radical Islam and an entire family of American nationalisms—could such movements have held our attention nearly so firmly *without* the affront of civilian blood, spilled so liberally? After all, this shift of focus has happened without our even trying; perhaps that is the truest testament to its profundity. No one this century in range of a router signal could have skirted the torrent of news and commentary on all things Islamic and populist. How can this flood, further swelled by the 2016 presidential election, be reckoned as anything other than a victory for modern terrorism and its truest believers, whose ideas, however opposed they are to each other's (and they are less opposed than it might seem), have never been so unignorable? In the long run of history, isn't that perhaps the most politically fertile result, whatever the associated costs to be borne in the near term?

Granted, much of this fame is more strictly infamy: mainstream coverage, especially of the noisier factions within the fundamentalist and populist movements, has naturally tended toward the negative. But has the very notion of the mainstream ever seemed so vulnerable, so lacking in gravitas? Besides, even this coverage has inevitably had to acknowledge what these radicals have gotten even a quarter-right about our many American betrayals, thereby surfacing many a defense of the essential justice of milder forms of these positions—forms that would simply be invisible, indeed, irrelevant, were it not for their fiery siblings. Surely this kind of conceptual ferment, out of which futures are distilled, can't be neatly negated by the concomitant losses—particularly those state retaliations provoked by violence against its civilian population, as they tend only, because of their outsize scale and vengeful tenor, to make the original transgression against noncombatants appear less obscene.

ANIMALS

Animal Liberation

Domestic breeds holding dominion over their lives—the thought cannot be denied a certain ethical appeal, however quixotic. Zoological gardens make the point well. They advantage the animals they house in vital respects, insulating them from threats they would face in the wild—disease, predation, starvation—just as we shelter our pets and farm animals from these dangers at home. Why is it, then, in making our way through even the most idyllic of zoos, we cannot shed the feeling that *nothing* genuinely belongs here, that the noblest garden can only be an empty one?

Are things actually any different with *human* being? Anyone knows that to founder neglected and unknown trumps flourishing merely by courtesy of another. Yet to *be* the one extending this courtesy, settling other beings into that amicable state of dependency we ourselves, if we have even a hint of dignity, smartly decline, gives the most peculiar satisfaction. Even when this authority is not so much as acknowledged, it exalts our relations with everything we have managed to tame; in a secular world, it might be one of the few enchantments left, making it easier to connive at its unseemly origins.

Could we wean ourselves from these paternal pleasures? Are we decent enough to want to? An obstacle remains in any case: domesticated creatures aren't much suited for life without our stewardship. Self-sufficiency is precisely what they have lost in the bargain. All the same, might it be best, however ugly we may find it, to let those creatures we have bred into helplessness fade from the Earth instead of indefinitely extending their dependency, keeping them confined in a kind of permanent childhood? When the two come apart, surely aesthetics must come second to ethics.

Would these species really vanish without our kindness? Or is our aegis less critical than we'd like to think, and nature more resourceful? Sterilization or conscientious observation could make the present generation of kept animals the last, while strays might be left to their own devices, as they are in many parts of the world—at least until their numbers become a trouble, at which point animal control might be selectively deployed. Many individual animals will perish in the streets, of course, but then most of them would otherwise simply have been executed at the local pound, hardly a grander fate.

Are there many domestic *breeds*, though, that with a bit of luck and opportunity would not reclaim their wildness in time, even if their numbers shrunk? Feral cats, packs of stray dogs, fugitive snakes—one finds these and many others in cities worldwide, proof that fauna may survive under the least organic of conditions. Of course, feral animals garner neither affection nor admiration from us, as pets and wild creatures do; yet through centuries of breeding, we are their true authors. Perhaps that is why their rediscovered autonomy affronts us. They didn't need us as much as we thought; the enchantment was empty.

Human Prey

Animal attacks vary profoundly in their moral significance. Problem sharks worrying a beach, say, differ from tigers and bears wandering into towns and maiming the folk. Limning the natural habitats of land animals is not without its vexations, particularly for creatures inhabiting the fringes of biomes; but being water-bound, sharks can almost never be taken to have strayed into human habitats, which are canonically terrestrial. *We* instead are the encroachers, as our reasons for entry serve no vital interest, at least not for the usual victims (the number of fishermen injured by sharks is vanishingly small; surfers and beach revelers are another matter). This is why the notion of putting down problem sharks discomfits.

When a bear crosses into a mountain village, things look different. Here too, of course, we have entered the animal's natural habitat. But we are equally within *our* natural range as a species. It would be incorrect to describe us as encroachers, and our grounds for retaliation are to that extent firmer. Compare this to a man's being mauled while camping in untrammeled wilderness. The moral pendulum swings back toward the bear; the camper, like the beachgoer, must accept without complaint the consequences of his recreation.

Smart Food

Living on flesh—the taking of life involved—haunts us in ways plant-eating doesn't. Next to the pitiless carnivore, the vegetarian cannot but be in the moral clear, we feel, and it is just this sort of peace-bringing that may entice us to take up the diet ourselves. But must we rue slaughtering animals more than harvesting most grains and vegetables, particularly where the death of the plant follows inevitably? (One wonders why only fauna can be slaughtered or massacred. No words of similar charge exist for the killing of flora.)

Animals have brains, of course, and hence consciousness, which brings with it capacities to suffer that plants cannot share in. But this would seem only to counsel that we slaughter animals swiftly and painlessly—a headshot to a deer, a bolt gun to a cow. Some will suppose that the moral gravity of sentience in this case inheres not just in any suffering we might inflict, but in those prospective pleasures we steal from them in bringing their lives to an early end. If only the future offered such guarantees. An animal's fate *might* hold pleasures, among them social or cognitive ones, but it might just as well turn gruesome and excruciating. Injury, disease, and neglect always lie in wait.

That headshot might well *save* our deer from a future rife with misery; we cannot say in advance.

If sentience cannot explain the trouble with painless killing, the killing must be the trouble. But on this score, plants are on all fours with animals. The plowing under of wheat, the uprooting of potatoes, and the picking of lettuce all end the lives of plants before they have run their course. Ultimately, to consume an organism, sentient or not, is to stand in the way of its flourishing. Perhaps this is the sturdiest criterion left: to possess a life, and with it a corresponding telos, endows what would otherwise be a mere thing with moral worth. Yet we have no reason to think that worth comes in degrees, that the ends of animals must be worthier of fulfillment than those of plants. The conclusion comes at once: the conscientious consumption of animals need not trouble us anymore than traditional agriculture.

Our presumption of a moral hierarchy among lifeforms may be grounded in nothing more than the desire that our killing preferences—when, what, and how—find rational sanction. That our sentiments, at least these ones, might be grounded only in habit, aesthetics, and anthropomorphic prejudice will strike some as repugnant. But perhaps it should be remembered that life is self-funding: the growth of organic matter depends on the destruction of other such matter. The thought that some biological forms are inherently worthier of prevailing in this struggle than others—that a human's life comes before a sheep's, and a sheep's before the grass on which it grazes—is unbecoming.

The Moral Kingdom

J. S. Mill's "hierarchy of pleasures" smoothly tracks our de facto parceling out of moral significance, regardless of the final justice of that distribution: the richer the pleasures a being can experience, the more importance we attach to its flourishing. A man in thrall to Schubert, a dog playing fetch with its master, a worm gnawing through mulberry leaves—these form a descending gradient of value. But pain is no less orderly than pleasure: a man, owing to his self-consciousness, can suffer with greater variety and depth than a dog, and a dog more profoundly than a worm. Preventing the first, then, seems more pressing than preventing the second; and the second more than the third.

All this comes with the usual *ceteris paribus* provisos, and quite often all else isn't equal. Take a bird pecking at the larva of a butterfly on the doorstep of extinction. Pitching a rock at the feathery thing seems natural and apt, even if there is every chance the impact will be mortal. The bird's pleasures and pains are likely richer than this would-be butterfly's, yet is killing it wrong? Surely not. We care about the survival of individuals; we care more about the survival of species, even the simplest ones.

FREEDOMS

Rights and Intervention

Once clear of the safe harbor of self-defense, justifying military intervention in other states' affairs usually goes by way of appeal to the sanctity of human rights. The United States, among other countries, appears to grant itself moral license to depose leaders or undermine rebels whenever they systematically commit or abet such transgressions against their own people. (Think of Libya, Egypt, Iraq, Bosnia, and so many other cases.) *Crimes against humanity* is the grandest of phrases invoked on the eve of such adventures; and it seems significant and nonaccidental that the purview of such crimes is left open, so that we might subsume new cases at will.

What might a principled threshold look like? The general abrogation of human rights? Which ones? Life must qualify if any do; liberty and happiness can't be far behind. If a state pervasively and selectively kills, confines, or injures innocent citizens, humanitarian grounds for intervention would seem to be firmly in place.

What else might such a principle license, though? After all, our own justice system deprives blacks of all these rights at a rate conspicuously disproportionate to the general population. Does this provide a justification to intervene in our affairs, on our streets, to any country mighty enough and sufficiently scrupulous about rights to carry it out? Is it only historical contingency, then, and not principle that shields us from this possibility?

Often it's not the government that commits the violations; it merely tolerates them within its borders. But a state unable, for whatever reason, to uphold basic rights among its citizens—a state, say, that can't stamp out widespread vigilantism and hence cannot ensure the self-determination of its people—would seem equally to give license for intervention to a morally scrupulous state or coalition.

There are also critical rights whose violation doesn't always or usually occur through the use of force. On the face of it, equality is as fundamental a right as any other. Might a society that systematically disenfranchises the indigent through de facto plutocracy, or that fails to secure the equal pay of women or the civil rights of transgender people, also invite intervention? Why should only violent crimes against humanity justify forcible intervention, and mere economic sanctions and the like be thought appropriate when rights violations are nonviolent or less sensational? What does this symmetry of means, pleasing as it may be, have to do with our grounds for intervention, which hinge not on *how* these basic rights are undermined but *that* they are at all?

Take the right not to be needlessly harmed: If a society inflicts widespread, chronic psychological distress on some class of citizens (the poor, women, the disabled), not through the application of physical force but by other means—simple ideological ones that brand such citizens second-class, say, if not a more formal apartheid—why should anyone demur at the notion that this right hasn't been respected and that it is this failure, even if it is an entirely bloodless one, that legitimates whatever intervention is necessary to correct it?

Recent American escapades in the Middle East and elsewhere prove, if it needed demonstrating, that it is easier to topple states than to mold them. But much of the history of empire involves just such methodical shaping, carried out over decades and centuries, inculcating an entire way of life among foreign peoples. If international human-rights interventions are inherently civilizing missions—and what are they, if they are not that?—we must reconcile ourselves to the implications: any society with the requisite where-withal, will, and rectitude could offer a rationale for remaking another in its own moral image; indeed, many in the past have done so, even if ulterior nonmoral motives (profit, for one) have ultimately invalidated the legitimacy of their actions.

Rational Force

We like to think of argument as coercion's foil. But isn't adducing decisive evidence for a proposition a way of compelling our assent to it, given that what we believe isn't under voluntary control in the way that bodily movement or the imagination is? Except for when the very idea of having *reasons* for belief is suspended (say, in matters of religious faith—but then should this even be called belief proper?) or the facts are irremediably murky (as in some matters of ancient history), what we believe is fixed not by our will but by our grasp of the relevant evidence. And to recognize *conclusive* evidence for a proposition is ipso facto to come to believe it, whether we like to or not.

That I believe, in 2020, that Donald Trump is the sitting U.S. president is not a choice I make. I am simply aware of far too much evidence that he is to believe otherwise. I cannot will myself into believing that, say, Joe Biden is president. I can *entertain* that counterfactual proposition, and I can, if I wish, imagine it in the minutest detail, as novelists do. But entertaining or imagining is not believing.

When someone attempts to persuade us of a claim, she must do so by proffering reasons to think it true, even if those reasons turn out to be spurious, and even if she knows them to be so and is only attempting to deceive us.

She may also rely on emotive tactics to make the evidence seem stronger than it really is. Yet it is at least the *appearance* of evidence and valid reasoning she must supply to change our minds. Which is to say, intellectual force operates in a distinctive way: you can't force someone to believe something in the way you can force him to the ground. Yet when we argue most successfully, our interlocutor isn't merely invited to change his mind, he is compelled to—by force of reason. Since the production of such arguments is a normative ideal of reasoning—would that all the claims we made were compelling—coercion in matters of belief isn't inherently problematic; whereas in the sphere of voluntary action, it cannot be but an obstacle to our ideals of autonomy.

Still, problems do lurk nearby. We all know opinionated sorts who would bully us with their ideas: the polemicist as intellectual thug. Rather than sympathetically bringing us around to their vantage, they try to make our claims look not just false but absurd, and their own the only remotely sensible ones on offer. Often, of course, they peddle flawed evidence to this end. Yet even then, if they manage to pass off their sophistry as sound argument, they can commandeer our convictions.

In the worst cases, not actually believing their own arguments, they prove well acquainted with the spuriousness of their speech; sometimes, they may even taunt us with this knowledge, drawing us into a quiet game of catch-the-fallacy. More frequently, though, they are no less deceived than we are, and their mistakes become ours through a sort of epistemic contagion, leaving all involved intellectually disfigured.

A Meaning of 'Free'

Doing as you please, satisfying your desires, is a basic strand in the fabric of freedom. To be free to do something in this sense is just to be able to do it should you want to; whereas you aren't free to do something that, even if you desire to, you cannot. The scope of your freedom will then be precisely limned by the range of desires, actual and possible, you are in a position to satisfy.

When thinking of freedom politically, discussion generally turns to external constraints, particularly the interference of other people, which amounts to infringement on your negative liberty. But the metaphysical notion of freedom doesn't necessitate distinguishing the various ways the satisfaction of our desires can be stymied, some of which have nothing to do with infringement. That you can't fly by flapping your arms, however much you may wish to—think of a very small child who may not yet realize the impossibility of it—is not a limitation on your capacities imposed by the interference of other people. All the same, there is a sense in which it's not something you're free to do, in that it's not a state of affairs you're capable of bringing about.

To be free in this sense—for your wishes to be satisfiable by actions you are able to undertake—is tantamount to being in control of yourself and your environment. The greater your control, in degree and in scope, the greater your freedom. However unethical it may be, Vladimir Putin is in a position to launch a large-scale invasion of Ukraine in a way very few of us are. In that respect he is freer than we are. (Not all freedoms are to be sought.)

What's nice about this sort of view of freedom is that it doesn't require us to be entirely, impossibly self-determining to be free. There's no need for us to have somehow chosen our basic character or psychological makeup. It's enough to be free and autonomous that our actions flow from, and often enough bring about the fulfillment of, the desires we have.

Compulsion or addiction complicates the picture. When you carry a pack-a-day habit yet you've not had a cigarette in a week (in an effort to quit), no one would describe your desperately lighting up as an action properly under your control. Just the opposite. What's gone wrong? You're not so much an agent of your desire but a hostage to it, and the proof is simple: though you want a cigarette terribly, you don't in the least *want* to want it. Acting autonomously is incompatible with such disavowing second-order desires, desires that express our sense of who we are, and who we are not. Where desires of the first and second order mesh smoothly, our selves remain cohesive; where they fall into conflict, we and our freedom begin to fray.

How to Defy

We're on intimate terms with *acts* of defying the ruling order: the George Floyd and Hong Kong protests, most recently, and the various Occupy movements and the Arab Spring a decade ago, to take a few instances. But there are less salient psychological *states* of defiance, too, and these might be more critical, for being more durable, than episodic eruptions of public discontent, which can induce a kind of moral catharsis that precludes lasting change. With our indignation discharged, returning to business as usual becomes emotionally easier, just as the weekend heals the wounds of the workweek so that we might go back to the selfsame toil on Monday. Even worse, perhaps, are the occasions when collective acts of defiance, often violent ones, *do* lead to decisive social changes; the twentieth century provides ample evidence that the cure can be worse than the disease.

Foucault wrote of how a "permanent critique of our contemporary age" might serve as an ethico-intellectual ideal, though he didn't fix the methodology of critique. This was wise, actually. It means that the notion of critique needn't entail a commitment to a pervasive hermeneutics of suspicion, even if Foucault and his heirs are often attracted to this paranoid approach. Instead, what we might treat as constitutive of critique is *cognitive* defiance. The details of this disobedience, though, must evolve alongside the societies that are its targets, so that they remain fit to reveal protean tensions and conflicts, functional and ideological, which switch guises from era to era. Such a spiritual condition may be a requisite for the most meaningful sorts of social change, or, at a minimum, of ongoing personal reformation, which shouldn't be underestimated in its downstream potential. Millions of local decisions taken independently but upon a common horizon certainly may have accretive effects. Admittedly, if all of that decision-making were shifted in the direction of a greater, defiant reflexivity, one wouldn't have much of a notion as to what particular social whole would emerge— the critical spirit can lead one to all sorts of places; one cannot specify them in advance. Yet one could be sure that society would be more deeply informed by scruples of every kind, which is a good in and of itself, as our pooled ratiocinative powers and all that flows from them would be put on firmer footing.

Taboos

Where there are pieties—and they are everywhere, even in ostensibly secular realms of society—there will be taboos. I still recall the baffled rage of the cosmopolitan intelligentsia that met the release, a decade ago now, of Jerry Fodor and Massimo Piattelli-Palmarini's *What Darwin Got Wrong*, a treatise that asked pointed questions concerning the soundness of evolutionary explanation, specifically the appeal to a mechanism of natural selection. The book's conclusions and premises may well be flawed, but there is nothing special in that. Thousands of wrongheaded books are released every year. The reaction, however, even in rarefied intellectual circles (including the *New York Review of Books*), was far more scornful, even contemptuous, than this garden-variety intellectual shortcoming can reasonably merit, given that the book was patently put forth in good faith by two venerable thinkers. Thomas Nagel's *Mind and Cosmos*, released two years later and also defending the notion that a Darwinian view of nature has its limitations, was derided and denounced rather than simply demurred at—a sure sign that respectfully questioning the explanatory power of evolution counts, in our era, as a kind of blasphemy. Now, more even-handed rebuttals to these books did eventually come, of course. But it is that initial tsunami of reactive hostility among the intellectual classes, who are trained to resist snap judgments, that bears remembering.

What is properly taboo is never self-evidently or seriously unethical. It would be bizarre to describe rape or genocide as taboo. Rather, taboos are tainted by persistent suspicions of a wrongness that is not easily demonstrable: habitual drug use and promiscuity are two that still hang on in polite society, though they have lost much of their power elsewhere. Others more closely comparable to the one with which we started include research into the genetics of intelligence, an area that is not intrinsically problematic—genes play some role in structuring all creatures' lives—yet tends to raise suspicions concerning motives (not always wrongly, either). Taboos exist in moral gray zones, places where our disapproval of a practice isn't matched by an argument against it that we ourselves regard as self-evidently true, much less others; hence our need, in shunning the practice despite this lack, to press our hostile emotions into service.

A genuinely secular society, it seems, would concern itself only with the most basic or vital ethical matters while excising its pieties and taboos, which are nebulous in comparison. Clearly we don't live in such a society. Yet one can take this conclusion in different ways. There are those who clamor for a social world liberated from taboo, one that countenances only rights violations and legal codes. But there are others. Might taboo and piety be features of the religious impulse *not* to be overcome, even for those who have no interest in upholding any particular religious tradition? Taboos express communal commitments that aren't essential to the very possibility of a stable society (as the prohibition on random murder is); hence they may not admit of knockdown arguments. Instead, in these realms, it may be affect and disposition that guide us, however uncertainly, rather than reason. A community that failed to be bound by these sorts of penumbral norms would not feel like much of a community at all, only a formal arrangement between strangers concerning fundamental rights. Yet the scope of ethics is greater than the scope of bare law, and it is in just this space where custom and taboo hold greatest sway. It is also where we test our imaginations against the bulwark of tradition: this, finally, is the appeal of the taboo, and it is why so much productive iconoclasm is predicated on its exploration. Without taboo, a certain kind of creative pressure dissipates, from which one can only expect a slackening of culture.

In Total Disbelief

Can I choose not to believe I'm typing this right now? If I've just indulged in angel dust, perhaps. But then maybe I'm *really* playing the piano, not typing. Who can say, if I'm out of my gourd, however temporarily? This doubt, of course, turns on my thinking that my perceptual capacities, owing to the drug, are impaired and thus untrustworthy. If I had no such belief—if I'd never decided to indulge—doubt could find no purchase, and I would find myself, quite passively, believing that I'm typing.

With Cartesian doubt, perceptual and reasoning capacities both come in for wholesale doubt. What allows for it? The *belief* that an evil demon might be toying with me. But then the doubt turns out not to be wholesale; and it is belief, of all things, that makes doubt possible.

Agency fares no better. How would intentional action be possible if I had no beliefs, no knowledge, about my surroundings, the state of my body, and especially the state of my mind, with all of its various intentions and desires and other attitudes? An entire infrastructure of belief underwrites the possibility of my so much as writing these words.

Free Jokes

The joke is a peculiarly flexible semantic act, in that the degree of seriousness with which we are meant to understand it is always an open question, and indeed can form part of the joke itself. Is it purely a non sequitur, funny only for its absurdity? Or is there more to it than that? Exactly how *much* more, though? In tackling uncertain ethical terrain, we often use the ambiguity of humor to advantage. The permanent possibility of disclaiming what has been said or done—"it was only a joke"—depending on the reactions of our audience, lets us float opinions and express sentiments we would never attempt in plain speech. With ordinary assertion, the sincerity of our utterances is conventionally taken for granted. There is no easy way of downshifting from the literal meanings of our words, no easy way, that is, of passing off our statements or insinuations as pretense made merely (or mostly, or partly) for pleasurable diversion and therefore not worth troubling over too much. In this way we may play with unfashionable notions without the usual risk of censure. Humor and freedom are thus related, and a society without any established practice of comedy would almost certainly be a less free one.

CITIES

Neighborhood Art

It can't be seriously doubted that graffiti sometimes bears the hallmarks of artistic achievement: formal skill, conceptual depth, emotive force. More controversially, some of this work must also be thought an enhancement to the cities of which they are a part, not entirely unlike the way in which sanctioned forms of public art sometimes (though hardly always) are. In many cities, there is a tacit embrace of street art, not in the tony parts of town, of course, but in stylishly shambolic quarters, which invariably end up tony soon enough. Spray-can work is admired in passing and even left to stand, at least when it isn't made over by artists with fresh visions for the block. (In less fashionable areas, of course, untouched graffiti represents municipal neglect rather than communal appreciation.)

One wonders, however, if such approbation neutralizes something vital to the original point of graffiti, which is in no small part to blight and disfigure. Formally, "street art" may resemble unsanctioned graffiti in all respects, but its mere acceptance as legitimate seems to steal a peculiar valence from it. Now and then, one sees crude graffiti executed in an upscale neighborhood, where it is manifestly unwelcome. Does it not visibly carry a social gravitas unmatched by more beautifully rendered work in an alley well known for its art, or on a length of stone wall airlifted to a museum for our decontextualized aesthetic enjoyment?

Much of graffiti's enhancing value, its vigor, emanates from its illicitness, the way that it disorders the streets and in so doing shows them to be more tumultuously alive than the harmonious, "enlightened" areas of town, where even the rebels, who have come for blood, are given a hand.

Part of what fixes the content, and hence the merit, of graffiti art involves factors that would not typically affect artworks that have been designed with gallery exhibition in mind. The viewing context is so much more varied—as it was with religious art of the past. Where exactly has the work been situated? How does its style and content not just interact with those surroundings—all art does that much—but how are they partly constituted by them, aesthetically, socio-politically, and so on? Finally, who is the work's primary audience? People who seek out these works for the experiences they afford? Or immediate residents who have no choice but to look, however they may feel about what they see? Unsponsored graffiti cannot be appreciated in a detached way, as easel painting of the last few centuries can. The very creation of such works is, in a direct sense, a necessarily political act.

Abstract Structures

If architecture were not a form of public art, the question of whether it has become overly academic would be less pressing. Most contemporary gallery art, after all, is deeply academic, if not always by design, then certainly in the manner it is received by audiences, long since trained to treat art as the organon of philosophy. This too is problematic, inasmuch as most of this work is hardly up to the task. But then no one demands that the public visit these galleries; if they like, they can always stick to the classical collections.

Architecture, being planted firmly in public space, offers no such relief, which makes its character all of our concern, not just the connoisseurs'. So many interventions in public life, when they come to have an academic aspect, suffer from the problem of a little knowledge: the half-baked neuro-babble we're subjected to (and speaking fluently) these days, with seemingly every aspect of human affairs receiving some quasi-evolutionary explanation, no matter how thin it stretches the core theory; or the economic metrics and findings we don't genuinely understand but feel compelled to speak to anyway. How many, for instance, have a plausible claim to grasping Thomas Piketty's research and the debate it stirred within the discipline of economics over wealth inequality (a debate that is not nearly as new as we suppose)?

We can ask, in this same spirit, how ideas born in certain quarters of the academy end up getting mangled in others (architecture departments), which in turn mangle public space. As with much recent gallery art, the appreciation of many newer buildings depends essentially on having a theoretical framework at hand to make sense of them. Without one, they can be alienating to look upon or walk through, to live in or work at. Consider all the edifices of previous generations in the International Style that remain, for many, a form of urban blight not stemming from the usual causes of poverty or neglect, but from the indulgence of philosophical ideas over appearances.

I myself worked for years in a Renzo Piano building in Manhattan that always left me cold and distanced, and this while having some sense for the deeper architectural aspirations of the age. There was, to begin with, far too much glass everywhere, glass where none was called for. Everything ran together. Months after I began working there, I asked a long-tenured colleague about it and was given to understand it was all simply a matter of transparency; the thought was built right into the place. Later I was to find him a true team player, a believer in what you might call compassionate surveillance. This notion, which I found it plausible to think the building embodied, regardless of Piano's intentions, didn't in fact raise my estimation of the building, even as it made it more intelligible. The intellectual values of clarity and directness had been turned, at this site, to foul ends, either by a theoretical mishandling (always possible) or, less generously, by design, marshaling philosophical talk hostile to solidity and presence, that urged instead for total penetrability by sight—which might suggest a total lack of obstacles—as a pretext for more sinister, labor-disciplining intentions.

The tower also had curious meshes floating above each of its faces, so whenever you looked at it from the street, you felt as if you were only half-seeing it, the way one does the entrance to a house through a screen door. There were *green* reasons for these screens—I could see this without being told or even grasping exactly what they did. This is how theory is lost in reception, without actually getting out of the way. Since most recent showpiece constructions of note had not opted for these unsightly shields that seemed to have been added on like overegged accessories, I could only assume there were ways of achieving environmentally sound results that didn't require them. Probably there was a tortuous aesthetic justification for the veil: something, I expect, about frustrating the urban gaze, never mind all the glass within.

More recently I have heard the building referred to as *lesser* Piano. I understand this.

Urban Languor

Metropolises are most vital just when our feeling for life is vaguest. When we are at our most alert, the bloom and buzz of the city can seem garish, ersatz, excessive in all the wrong ways. It is then that we crave the country, or even the maligned suburbs, precisely for their emptiness, which is as much psychological as physical. Into this space we may extend ourselves without impediment. Everything is up to us—the purest freedom when we have the spirit for it, and an anxious-making obligation when we don't. Then, invariably, it's back to the city, to be impressed by it once again, compensating for our own insufficiency by taking on its shape and substance until some semblance of interiority, a soft stirring of the will, returns to us a need for self-origination the city all but precludes, which must again be satisfied only through departure.

STATES

A Global Citizenry

We are often asked by social progressives to think of ourselves as global citizens. But is citizenship the sort of thing one can simply think one's way into? As a political concept, citizenship requires certain basic social institutions to be in place to make it possible: that is, to be a citizen is to be a citizen of some *polis* or other.

Lacking a world state, or single sovereign authority, global citizenship is from the start a confused notion. It's why we are asked to *see ourselves* as world citizens rather than actually become such, as one does of a state. But even the metaphor of citizenship is inapt. Being a citizen has little to do with one's ideals or conduct; it's why criminals and dissidents don't ipso facto lose their citizenship. It has instead to do with which politico-legal rights one has secured or been accorded, and which sovereign authority one is answerable to (and owed protection by) in the first instance. Naturally, the substance of these rights and restrictions varies from place to place, since each political body mints its citizens to its own standards: the United Kingdom's lack of a codified constitution with special legal priority is one of the many ways in which Britons differ essentially from Americans. Yet the concept of citizenship itself shows unity, issuing directly from a sovereign's relationship to its subjects.

Things being so, there may come a time when international law, so far only sporadically enforced, incomplete in scope, and undersubscribed, cannot be flouted by states or persons without incurring profound and lasting penalties. When its rulings have that kind of bite, and the laws it stipulates are substantive and meticulously applied, global citizenship will become an intelligible notion. For now, though, we must make do with a more serviceable idea: being globally conscious citizens of local poleis.

Good Observation

Ceteris paribus, surveillance extracts better behavior from us. With someone watching over our shoulders—or just the threat of someone's so doing—temptation evaporates. Empirical studies are hardly required here. Plato's Ring of Gyges suffices.

What sort of ethical difference does observation's taming of behavior make, though? Certainly fewer ignoble acts occur, and that utilitarian truth must count for quite a lot. But if the only thing preventing you from doing wrong is the likelihood of being caught, it is prudence, not rightness, driving your actions. It is behavior under Ring-of-Gyges conditions, where your deeds are untraceable—and not utility—that matters to morality qua character. Which is only to say the virtuous behave themselves whether or not anyone is looking; and a world in which people behave for reasons of goodness must be superior to a world in which, we might suppose, there are no more immoral acts committed, yet such is achieved only through prudential reasoning and the deterrent of surveillance.

Perhaps prudence is all that liberal states can reasonably expect from their citizens. They build only the thinnest of moral outlooks into the law or public life generally, just enough to sanctify liberty, democracy, and hence their own legitimacy. As a consequence, modern democracies don't have much purchase on their subjects' hearts; they aren't aligned with their citizens' worldviews in any but the shallowest sense. A prudential attitude to citizenship seems a natural partner to this managerial conception of the state. So long as the referee—the state—doesn't cite you for an infraction of the ground rules, you are free to commit yourself to an ethic of your own. The best we can do, under such conditions, is to make our referee as close to omniscient as possible, so that infractions don't go unnoticed. Expecting citizens to obey an honor code, which is what morality proper requires, is simply asking too much.

Of course, a less disenchanted politics is possible, provided we can meet its spiritual rigors. The state would need to trade its referee's whistle for a coach's playbook; it would need to take sides and positively back a rich and particular conception of social life, and of justice, so that subjects come to see cheating the state as tantamount to cheating themselves.

Patriots

When it comes to identity, love of country is nearly always the fraught question, not love of city, province, or continent. Many who are content to say they love their city without reservation are more than a little reluctant to say the same of their country. This must tell us something about politics, the art of government: it is at the level of the state—the sovereign body—that the dangers of loving one's place manifest most vividly. Wars, economic sanctions, and other hostile acts directed toward political bodies are typically executed at this level, and governmental approval can suffice to set these processes in motion, without any consultation with or approval from more comprehensive organizations like NATO, the European Union, or the UN. By contrast, provinces follow the lead of the states of which they are a part when it comes to initiating aggression of any kind against other political entities, or even forming most kinds of relations with them.

Love of country cannot but clear a path to jingoism, which is a kind of abuse of sovereignty, as well as the central reason to fear unqualified patriotism. If city-states with standing militaries were still common in the world, some of us—the same ones who are on guard against patriotic excess—would surely be less comfortable with the casual chauvinism embodied in bromides like "[Hometown] is the greatest city in the world!" These are just the sorts of sentiments that can lead to politically reckless actions. It is only because cities are obedient to the countries of which they are a part and don't bear ultimate responsibility in matters of territorial defense that we feel such expressions are harmless. But that is an entirely contingent matter, and it is worth recognizing it as such.

That is the question of loving one's *state*. What about loving one's *nation*, which is just that shared sense of community, values, and history between persons that exists in most stable states around the world? Where no robust sense of nationhood obtains, there is little to bind people of the territory together, and any state that stakes it claim there will live under the shadow of secession, perhaps many times over, until the fragments begin to limn nations.

While the idea of loving your town or even your city is fathomable, loving your country, which may consist of hundreds of millions of people dispersed over tens of millions of square miles, is as hopelessly vague as mentally picturing a million-sided figure. What would love amount to here? Certainly something far more abstract than love of a town, or indeed of a person, which is more concrete still. I find it easy enough to love my neighborhood, which amounts to a few city blocks, nothing like a town or a city. The scale is perhaps ideal for real understanding to take hold. Over the course of a half dozen years, I've come to know every inch of that little territory, its shops and restaurants and subway stops, its hotels and movie houses, and, of course, partly through this, its residents, whom I can usually distinguish from mere passersby, and whom I subtly acknowledge throughout my day. A few blocks to the east or west, north or south? They are not just farther away but more distantly known and felt; and farther out from there, any sense of intimacy quickly falls away.

There's an exception to this logic of distance, however, that may vindicate more diffuse forms of love by making them tangible to us. Though we might never have a distinct feeling of affection for our country or its people as a whole while we're in it, when we come into contact with a countryman of ours abroad, often we do feel something like it, particularly if we've encountered some sort of difficulty in our travels, or we find the local culture alien. How often then do we find ourselves unthinkingly aligning ourselves with any compatriot at hand, however little we may resemble him! He might in fact be just the sort we'd be quick to tire of back home, but here things are different. A formal unity—the two of us bound by the same passport, sharing the outline of a life at least—is just what we seek when things go pear-shaped.

Social Renewal

In politics, the thought of beginning anew, skirting the various historical precedents that inform the times—any time—can hold a curious appeal, especially in eras of boundless turmoil, like ours. Yet there are reasons to resist this kind of ahistorical thinking, not least because social memory provides the map, always unfinished, but no less a map for that, of known political possibilities. Taking up the amnesiac's stance toward our prior lifeways amounts to tossing out all the experimental data we have: all the many ways of coordinating human lives that *haven't* turned out well, of course, but also, among all these negative results, little glimmers of the good life. To proceed as if the past were baggage best shed in the interests of a new future would not merely leave us vulnerable to pointlessly reexperiencing other ages' failures, whose worth today consists in indicating which regions of this map of political space can be x-ed off as unfit for life; equally, such dismissiveness cuts us off from the redemptive potential of history—the fact that it has not *all* been folly, that deep within the muck and mire there are diamonds to be plucked.

WARS

War and Peace

Often we are too quick to wage war. A good number of violent conflicts around the world might have been forestalled by steadier and more measured diplomacy, carried out in earnest not only on the brink but long before. All the same, the notion that every international dispute has a "talk" solution carries no conviction.

In the gravest matters of politics, agreeing to disagree is not an ethical option: nuclear weapons testing, the profligate burning of fossil fuels, the commission of genocide, the occupation of another's land. Not every dissonance can be allowed to go unresolved; part of finding genocide an abomination is the willingness to do what one can to prevent it. And where discussion and debate fail to resolve such disputes, a judiciously fought war can sometimes be the most ethical solution to hand. (Doing nothing may well be worse.)

Of course, enforced political resolutions won't last. But then, what resolution does? As positions, interests, technologies, ideologies, and fortunes mutate, diplomatic fixes are just as liable to come undone. Yet that doesn't undermine their value: what they grant is *reprieve* from the exigencies of our disputes, not an abolishment of them.

Nothing short of a meteor strike (or possibly just climate change) could provide that.

It also shouldn't be forgotten that war does other things for us. The bourgeoisie were invigorated by the prospect of battle on the cusp of the First World War. They volunteered in great numbers, they fought with brio, and everything ended in shellshock. Yet sustained harmony bores us. It's true in music and the other arts, too: happiness writes white, to paraphrase a Frenchman. Nothing quickens the pulse like conflict.

Cooperation and Catastrophe

Occasionally global threats to humanity neutralize the usual skirmishing between nations. World War Two shows as much. Really it shows more than that: a threat to the survival of humanity isn't needed to induce this conditional unity. A threat merely to the survival of humanity as we know it suffices. The plausible fear that Axis rule over much of Europe and East Asia might fundamentally rewrite longstanding social and political norms compelled the Allied nations to quash their many conflicts of interest and act in concert. (Near the end of the war, a genuine global existential threat would emerge, of course. Nagasaki and Hiroshima were its calling cards.)

This was not an erasure so much as a suspension of national divisions, lasting only as long as the emergency itself. The ancient cross-purposes and resentments between the Allies took no time in resurfacing just after the Axis powers surrendered. A really durable crisis, though, might bring about a suspension so lasting it might go proxy for an erasure.

Climate change fits this bill: an exigency that over the next century or two will, by all accounts, evolve into a global flashpoint not unlike a world war, requiring the pooled efforts of the world's nations, working collectively rather than competitively, to conduct triage in the face of pervasive humanitarian catastrophes involving famine, natural disaster, resource scarcity, technological inadequacy, and asylum seeking—all on an unprecedented scale.

For now, the worst of the climate crisis is far ahead of us, and if history is any guide, without an imminent or ongoing calamity of global scale, intergovernmental cooperation is unlikely to be forthcoming. As it is with cigarette smoking in one's youth, the symptoms for most of us now are relatively mild. When our agonies are manifest, and living tragedy induces angry and terrified peoples to speak and act as one, it will, unfortunately, be others' lives at stake and not ours, most of us being long since departed. The immediate costs of climate change won't offset our absorption in national self-interest for some time yet. But once it begins to, the vastness of planetary timescales ensures that the period of earthly emergency will last far longer than a world war—as will, one presumes, the era of panicked global cooperation so induced.

Blood and Honor, or American Carnage

The suppression of explicit war photography from the public is sometimes justified on the grounds that it is disrespectful to the soldiers to display just how they became casualties, and equally, it seems, just how they inflicted casualties on the opposition. But how did injury and death, the very lifeblood of armed conflict, become something from which civilians must avert their eyes, for—of all things—the sake of the soldiers? One would think notions of heroism and glory are served best precisely by bearing witness to the costs borne by soldiers, both the wounds they sustain and the ones they inflict.

The few soldiers I have known personally had no qualms about civilians seeing just what happens to them or others on the battlefield. But perhaps they were grittier than most. Suppose soldiers by and large do have qualms about it. What would it prove? Surely their preferences wouldn't conclusively settle the question of what we *ought* to be seeing, as civilians financing armed conflicts.

Justifications proffered for withholding battle footage smack of bad faith. There is generally not much clamor for more unvarnished war reportage from the public, and almost none at all when the war is domestically popular. We needn't weave baroque explanations for this fact when the simplest one is also the most plausible: a more intimate exposure to the prosecution of war simply isn't wanted, no more than a close look at the factory farm that stocks our meat aisle is. We can put it even more strongly: war's remaining a hazy, far-off thing is something positively desired by many of us, even if we don't frame it that way to ourselves.

There is something right in the simple thought that if you are too squeamish to peek in the slaughterhouse that produces your dinner, you may need to reconsider your diet. By the same logic, if the sight of war's carnage strikes you as unbearably grim, instead of looking the other way on the pretext of honoring the soldiers, perhaps you should be less supportive of the government's sending them into harm's way to carry out these deeds on your behalf. There is nothing more disrespectful, really, than glossing over the realities of war.

The Killing Interest

What would you kill for? Self-defense is a trivial answer for all but pacifists. But what about enlisting in the military, where killing is more or less in the job description, or joining law enforcement, where suspects and convicts are not infrequently killed by officers.

I have no friends or family in the military or police, so it never occurred to me to consider a profession requiring the willingness to apply lethal force. Thinking about it now, though, I can't see myself volunteering for such a job. Not that I think the use of force, including the mortal kind, isn't necessary at times. Or that the values of my society aren't worth killing (and dying) over. If there were no one else to pull the trigger, I am sure that I would. But so long as there are others to do the job, why would I *choose* to be the executioner?

Why would *anyone* want this kind of work? Is there not a sense that, morally speaking, it should only be undertaken out of necessity? There are, for instance, countries that require all men of a certain age to serve for a time in the military, to distribute this social and moral burden equally. Such a system seems to me perfectly fair and just (you could subject women to the same requirement if your sense of fairness demands it). What is curious is that many countries, including the United States, have no need for such a policy: they can raise large standing armies and police forces on a volunteer basis alone, even though nearly all of those volunteers are capable of making a living wage in another line of work. Evidently that work is, for them, more odious than becoming the hatchet man. At the right price—military and police compensation is substantial— some of us would rather kill than, say, work in retail or construction.

Some may simply be indifferent to the nature of the job. As far as they're concerned, it's a way of making a nice living, even getting a college education paid for, that by the bye involves killing. Others, sad to say, lured by the thrill of authority and the rush of violence, are in it not in spite of the killing but because of it. Whether this should trouble us less or more than the "accidental" soldier who enlists merely for the dental plan and the cheap travel is not easy to say.

Others again, though, may find honor in being the ultimate guarantors of a social order and a way of life, which mere words cannot achieve. The true resiliency of a state, now and always, lies in its facility in summoning death. Perhaps there can be a kind of grace in seeking out the dirty work.

NATURES

Denying the Obvious

Have climate-change deniers become, by this point, nearly as perverse as those who claim the Holocaust is a historical fiction? There is the heinousness of the actual events to consider, of course. But there is also the *epistemic* heinousness of the denials. On the first matter, it's clear enough that actions deliberately incurring great human costs—and the killing of innocents must count, if anything does—are more repugnant than actions only incidentally doing so, even if this effect is entirely foreseen (as with much collateral damage in war). We don't burn fossils fuels for the purpose of putting the Maldives underwater or compromising the lives of future generations. They suffer instead as a byproduct of our energy gluttony. By contrast, Germany's National Socialists exterminated Jews *for the purpose* of exterminating them. Their death was no side effect.

The number of lives climate change ultimately extinguishes or prevents from coming into being, given our current carbon appetite, will likely be much greater than six million, even if the harm is dispersed over many miles and many years. Which is worse: a limited, deliberate annihilation of life, or a much broader, unintended siege on humanity that cumulatively dwarfs it in scale? There is no point pretending there is tidy answer available, but this, anyway, is the question.

Regarding the denials themselves: to say the Holocaust is a fabrication is effectively to deny the reality of the past. Despite the Germans' attempt to destroy all trace of their operations in the last months of World War II, it's hard to imagine a semi-clandestine event for which we have such a large trove of preserved evidence: the infrastructure of the camps (some of which have been turned into memorials and museums), the endless piles of bones in mass graves, the ovens full of human ash, and all the many contemporary records of it written by both the Nazis and the Jews (and many others). If all this is a candidate for sincere doubt, what chance does the more distant past stand? Surely the evidence for, say, the French Revolution's reality couldn't be any stronger than this.

As for denying that human activity is a leading driver of increases in global temperatures in the Anthropocene, whether through the burning of fossil fuels, the clearcutting of forests, the raising of cattle, or the introduction of particulate matter into the upper atmosphere through air travel, we must ultimately defer to empirical geoscientific research. The nature of the evidence for the causal links is quite technical in nature, and most of us are in no position to appraise it. Not so with recent events like the Holocaust: one needs no special historiographical training to appreciate much of the bountiful evidence, which still includes living testimony.

For these reasons, denying widely documented historical events must stand as even more preposterous, and pernicious, than rejecting even very well corroborated experimental findings in the natural sciences. It makes some sense, then, that the worst a climate-change denier will face is ridicule and derision; his Holocaust counterpart, in many countries, will end up in prison for his trouble.

Ecological Dissonance

Naturalists sometimes suggest that human beings are a singularly rapacious bunch, the only creatures whose drives have led them into a state of self-destructive disequilibrium with their environment. Doubtless we're frequently responsible for unbalancing ecologies. White-tailed deer have experienced runaway growth in the United States, as we have both cleared forests for farmland, inadvertently creating ideal habitats for them, and killed off the wolves and cougars that are their natural predators. Asian carp introduced into American waters have destroyed species native to Lake Michigan and other water bodies. Yet long before even the first hominids emerged, frequent shifts in the environment—melting glaciers, rising mountains, atmospheric vicissitudes—routinely undermined stable ecologies and drove profound changes in plant and animal populations, including many more species extinctions than the Anthropocene has witnessed.

Still, as the planet's only moral agents, it is our distinctive human responsibility, so long as we accept the ultimate dignity of life in all its variousness, to give succor to other extant beings and species when we can, and especially when they are on the brink of extinction—*not* because the world and its current ecological shape are morally worthier than the worlds of one hundred thousand or one million years ago, with their rather different array of species, but because it is the world we find ourselves in, and so the only one in which we may give aid.

The Mind, In Illness and In Health

A cursory look at the five editions of the *Diagnostic and Statistical Manual of Mental Disorders*, issued over the past sixty years, shows the border between illness and health, when it comes to the mind, to be protean.

This is not the dirty secret of psychiatry; it is its first and founding truth. The more one delves into the modern psychiatric literature, tracing to mid nineteenth-century German neurological research, the more obvious it becomes that all the field's significant practitioners and theoreticians began from the premise that diagnosis and treatment in psychiatry involves unique difficulties. Yet the profusion of hard cases and the scarcity of outright cures cast no doubt on the discipline's basic medical efficacy, even if the amelioration of psychiatric conditions often requires a battery of therapies and more than a little trial and error.

Granted, sharply distinguishing a merely somber disposition from dysthymia will likely always be a fool's errand; it will also always be the sort of case skeptics lean on. Yet the task is remarkably simpler when major depression is at issue: struggling to get out of bed and succumbing to frequent bouts of tears for many months isn't compatible with robust mental health on anyone's understanding, even if it may be perfectly natural for someone to become like this under unusually trying circumstances, like the death of a child. The same holds for garden-variety moodiness in comparison to pronounced forms of bipolar disorder, and for serious personality disorders, too. The notion, popular with some Foucauldians, that pathologizing certain states of mind can be a form of social control or exclusion is a potentially useful idea in dealing with cases at the periphery: there needn't be anything wrong with being somber or aloof; nor should the capricious and skittish always be "cured" of their volatility. But this approach holds no water for grave, paradigm conditions that cause disabling distress and undermine a person's capacity to carry out their own projects, which is part of what it means to be an agent at all.

In these unambiguous instances, of which there are many and upon which the case for psychiatry must ultimately be mounted, the value of drug, talk, and behavioral therapy cannot be gainsaid, whatever social component may be involved in the classification of mental disease (and surely there is one, as cultures carve up the spectrum of mental health and illness in their own ways). The idea that cognitive therapy hasn't helped anyone reconceive their lives in more hopeful terms, or that lithium, Thorazine, and Prozac haven't materially altered outcomes for those in the grips of bipolar disorder, psychosis, and severe chronic depression is difficult to credit.

All of which is to say, gray zones abound in psychiatry. But there is plenty of black and white in the picture, too.

FUTURES

The Life or the Work

At one time or another, most of us have wondered whether the routine undertakings of life—office jobs, marriage, children—have stood in the way of more exalted futures. Yet for every accomplished artist or athlete or activist who trades away some part of the ordinary satisfactions of life for the extraordinary ones, thousands of others try the same and end up worse for it. The trouble, of course, is that you'll usually discover whether your achievements, even in your own eyes, are significant enough to offset the compromises made in other areas of life only *after* the point of no return, when there's no longer anything you can do to salvage the situation, no more chances to make a good living or be a decent father to your children.

Karl Marx notoriously neglected his filial duties in the interests of his intellectual labors, which were genuinely prodigious. Whereas the case of Paul Gaugin's choice of the work over the life is murkier—could he really have become both a great painter *and* a passable family man?—it is not so unreasonable to suppose, I think, that Marx might not have had the fortitude to write and research in such an all-consuming way while properly tending to his more worldly duties.

Though he would have had his hopes, Marx obviously

couldn't have known the profound effect he would have on world history, nor the sheer intellectual magnitude of his oeuvre, when he set to work on the questions of political economy. Many other European political theorists and economists were working around the same time, with results that were decidedly more modest. Take Marx's German contemporary Wilhelm Roscher, a founder of the now long-out-of-fashion historical school of economics, whose works have not held up nearly as well as Marx's. All the same, he was certainly influential in his lifetime and in the half-century to follow. Countless others appeared in the periodicals of the nineteenth century who were not of much account in their own time *or* ours, though some of their prospects would have once seemed as auspicious as any of their peers'.

Ultimately, this is the lot of most who attempt creative endeavors, whether in art, politics, science, business, or so many other things; most results are exceedingly modest, and few of these projects will have much significance at any point, often to anyone, including the initiators themselves. Hence any serious compromises made in the name of these gambits will go unredeemed: the world, and usually they themselves, will be worse off for their loftiness.

All this means is that it's rarely *reasonable* to live single-mindedly. But some always will, and among them a few will come out ahead, by great margins even. Certainly the rest of us are in some way grateful to them, since we are the beneficiaries of their abandonment of common duty. Retrospectively, though, can we ever wholeheartedly give our blessing to their choice, in light of the badness of the bet?

Tomorrow's Strangers

Caring about humanity's far future doesn't hinge on whether our descendants share our way of life, residing in communities informed by similar mores. But it may depend on their *not* organizing themselves in ways we find repellant. If it seemed as though certain technological or environmental developments had in all likelihood put human life on a return course to widespread autocratic governance, and that democracy were merely an aberration, it is hard to see how that would not weaken our concern for distant future generations, so long as there was nothing we could do to give ourselves reasonable hope of altering the situation. The same goes for abject environmental catastrophes that are to come hundreds of years from now; if there isn't much of a long-range future to speak of, not for humanity, anyway, we will have no need to consider them.

There would still be the near future to worry over, though. No one of any moral capacity can fail to concern himself with the fate of at least the children and grandchildren of his generation. Partly this may be owing to sheer temporal proximity, which doubtless effects our sentiments even when it makes no intellectual difference. But it must also be because we know our actions will tangibly—indeed, relatively predictably—reverberate through the lives of those who immediately follow. It is the salience of these causal links that precludes indifference.

Living Without Limit

There are technologists who believe, not incredibly, that within a couple of centuries, machine-driven, posthuman immortality may be possible for the wealthiest of us. Beyond the novelty of it, though, is it actually something worth seeking? Assuming the immortality in question has an escape clause—your psychological continuity will be extended into the future as long as you care for it to be— then I suppose at a certain age, when you're short of natural time, you might be inclined to give it a try, particularly if there are loose ends that need tying up (children to finish raising, books to finish writing); or there are prospective experiences that only show up on the horizon, beyond the border of your natural lifespan; or if vast stretches of your life have been lost to missteps, and you're in search of lost time.

Anti-aging gene therapies may be with us much sooner; at that point, they may let us arrest the aging process at a stage of our choosing. If you are a poet or a mathematician, couldn't you use a few decades as a twenty-five-year-old, when your powers are in full bloom? If you are an athlete, wouldn't you be tempted to arrest your physical development around the same age and spend the next years cleaning up against the less experienced and the over-the-hill?

The chief threat to agelessness is simple boredom. Can you keep yourself meaningfully occupied for a thousand years? How about a hundred thousand? Eternity? Our imaginations are subject eventually to diminishing returns, some much sooner than others. But whose wouldn't give out after a millennium? And it is at just that point that human life becomes gratuitous, a chore you'd rather not draw out.

Gender in the Twenty-Second Century

The last several decades have seen a manifest unmooring of gender difference from sexual difference. All evidence suggests it will continue, and that must be to the good; the clusters of values that have long traveled under the headings of masculinity and femininity have been found to float free of sex, and therefore need justifying in some other manner. But this development does not suggest which among these values we ought to uphold and which we might better abandon. Certainly the changes haven't been equitable: it's mostly women switching to trousers and blazers, not men switching to dresses. The erasure of gender and the push toward a more unisex approach to selfhood has led to a general masculinization of culture and a shrunken role for many of the values canonically associated with femininity: patience, grace, and empathy; indirection and discretion; the heart to suffer and sacrifice without complaint; a recognition of the centrality of shame and guilt to our emotional lives; and more generally, *delicacy* and *restraint* in all their many forms (as against their prime agonist, *transparency*). Twentieth-century masculine norms have metastasized, becoming fundamental values for all now: an unabashed assertiveness mobilized in the efficient and informed optimization of one's experience. This is a life lived by blunt force.

Men have changed too, no doubt. They spend time in the home, they pay attention to their children and wives; they cry more often and more publicly; they worry about their clothes and grooming more. Few men today would be regarded as *men* by Americans of the 1950s or even the 1980s. Yet, for all that, the shift women have made toward masculine norms is patently far greater, and more pervasive, than the reverse, which has come at some loss of balance in the values of the culture.

Once upon a time, lipstick feminists did try to recover some of those devalued norms—whether they focused on the most vital ones is debatable—but this wasn't enough to correct the general tilt toward masculine virtues. Whether it takes a decade or a century, one hopes the full range of those fallen values will be fully restored and in fact raised in esteem, this time for women and men both. It will be easy to know the day has come: for one, the presidential campaigns of women won't require them to ape men to make headway.

The Fate of the Humanities

At august universities, the ones with monumental endowments and inordinate pride, the economic future doesn't look all that different from the past, the coronavirus pandemic notwithstanding. The same can't be said for their poorer cousins. It's become clear in these last decades that the great bulk of institutions of higher learning can no longer mimic their tonier counterparts in exalting the humanities, which both cost more to fund on a per-student basis, given their smaller enrollments, and attract far less outside investment than the applied and basic sciences do. As economic realities ossify, a shift away from the high-minded liberal arts toward more practical, profitable programs—to wit, the business, communications, and journalism majors that have infiltrated academe during the last century—is now well underway.

Infiltration may be an unhappy analogy, though. *Should* a university education be indifferent to vocational training? Should *episteme* and *techne* be held apart? That suited the old guard, of course, whether the aristocracy or the haute bourgeoisie, much as the separation of fine art from craft did during the seventeenth and eighteenth centuries. It was a mark of luxury that both learnedness and fine art were *not* wedded to the material concerns of life, but instead functioned as sources of abstract, contemplative value. If we have managed over the last hundred years to surmount the alienation of art from craft—no longer is it assumed that artworks serving a social or moral purpose must be diminished by that—we are still learning to do the same with knowledge and technical skill, by coming to recognize that forms of understanding springing from and fastening to the skilled performance of the essential tasks of practical life are, if anything, lent further value through that link rather than corrupted by it.

Could it be a sign of political progress, then, that education is ever more answerable to lived life and concrete benefit? The ebbing of the so-called gentleman's education as the template for higher learning might be reckoned a liberation from an unduly aestheticized conception of knowledge.

That's not to say the humanities have no place in the curriculum. It is rather a question of what should stand at the center of an education and what at the periphery. Must we lament the reversal that is taking place at so many universities: the gradual decentering of generalist majors like philosophy and history and the growing importance of vocationally oriented ones? Does this represent a regression of the culture, as many fear, or simply the progressive overcoming of the valorization of impractical knowledge?

The Arc of Poetry

Where will poetry be, fifty years hence? It's hard not to think that the tradition stretching from Homer all the way through Paul Muldoon will be even less relevant than it is today. It is already so narrowly confined within the culture, though, that if it gets any narrower it might just disappear from common sight.

A more optimistic view would find some hope in social media, the widespread usage of which suggests that our appetite is strong for condensed expression, the very heart of lyric poetry. Might Twitter and text messaging serve as beachheads in reestablishing verse as a cultural force in the decades ahead? Only so long as we mean *verse* in a sense that is at some distance from the tradition. Most contemporary poetry is nothing if not oblique—too oblique to command broad interest, not least because the curriculum, for good or bad, no longer assumes verse's fundamental place in an education. The skills needed to decipher most formal poetry simply aren't possessed by many.

We would instead be in the realm of folk poetry, which has little connection to learning. This will please some and not others. Is there a middle course to consider? Digital culture's tendency toward speed and brevity in discourse might well lead to an expansion in the audience for poetry, at least of a direct, topical form that is complementary to social media discourse. Already a younger generation of populist-leaning poets, ones who have some knowledge of poetics but are keen to practice an artful forgetting in the name of inclusion, suggest that such an expansion is in the offing. The extent to which this kind of verse might serve as a bridge to more elliptical poetry is unclear, though the rebirth of a non-academic audience might narrow the gap some by drawing even high-minded poets, who would no longer be restricted to speaking with their peers, toward greater immediacy and emotional power, which needn't conflict with formal complexity.

This might all be wrongheaded, of course, and the very question of poetry's cultural relevance might not be worth troubling over. Since literacy, scholarship, and fine writing were once the preserve of nobles and clergymen, there's nothing odd in poetry's returning to its ancestral home among sophisticates, now that the wider culture has far less taxing diversions available to it, ones that don't require reading at all. What we may really find hard to imagine, decades from now, is that broad swathes of the culture ever bothered with things as fussy as *Childe Harold's Pilgrimage* or *The Age of Anxiety*.

Uncertain Labors

Before the rise of the precariat, the story of work was simpler. In the post-war era, it was the single enterprise—often the single company—you dedicated your life to outside the home. It satisfied material needs, yes, but it also furnished a stable self-conception via collective goals, an articulated community, and a set of milestones with which to measure out your progress through life. Socializing the young to the working world entailed showing them the different kinds of people they might become, the sorts of long-term commitments they might undertake. Keeping in the black, which seems the very definition of working life now, was then only an element.

You could say the job has triumphed over the career, the episode over the story. Anyone entering the workforce knows this implicitly, the torturous sense of freedom now suffusing our lives. The ancient dream of liberty, the conquest of destiny, has been realized, in its way, and nothing could torment us more. For precariousness is both an economic and psychological condition, and by this point it is baked into the very idea of work. Stable livelihoods, selves with a telos, were once a birthright, or at least a practical ideal; now they are slipping beyond the pale of the imagination.

There is at least some good in this. A less structured self and world puts everything up for grabs: if failure is now permanently imminent, so is success—the old need to steadily abide the protocols of career progress is irrelevant for the fateless. Anything might work; anything might fail. The amorphousness of our working lives has another benefit: what we do to survive no longer necessarily says much about who we are. To ask someone what he does for a living with the idea of learning something essential about his character is almost quaint today. One *does,* or might do, a lot of things. But what one cares about? This question now commands our attention in its own right, having been disentangled by the historical moment from distinct matters of labor and livelihood.

Regressive Innovation

The cultural idée fixe of innovation presents newness as an end in itself, quite apart from any improvements to human life made possible by the innovated technologies. Even if their appeal has peaked, electronic books have succeeded in taking a fifth of the market away from their paper rivals, though they are manifestly less pleasant to read, notate, and navigate, on top of not costing substantially less than most softbound versions. Periodicals in digital formats have done far more damage to print sales, and while they are generally cheaper, the tradeoff in the quality of the reading experience is palpable. Something just as plain holds for twenty-first-century transitions from optical discs to streaming music and video technologies. You don't need an expert eye or ear to perceive the falloff.

In what sense, then, are these recent innovations *improvements* on their predecessors? Clearly they aren't experiential improvements. No, the improvements must be found elsewhere, principally in cost and ease: one can now more conveniently and cheaply take in a greater number of books, magazines, records, and films. But granting this obvious truth is not actually granting much, even if we often treat it as if it were and simply go ahead swapping out the old for the new. The question we've not yet posed is both obviously germane and generally ignored—and not only in this sector of economic life: do these technologies represent *all-things-considered* improvements? After all, *that* is the only kind that can justify the switch. And it is just here where our path grows rocky. For is it an ironclad law that a greater diversity of low-grade experience invariably trumps a smaller range of the high-grade sort? Nor is the reverse the case, either. If you continually shrink the sphere of your richest experiences, surely you'll come to a point where you'll find more worth in a greater bulk of somewhat thinner experiences: a single film displayed in the highest possible definition isn't patently more valuable than ten movies with a touch more pixilation (though how *much* more certainly matters). Hence every technological innovation must be appraised in light of our total conception of advancement, and not merely against that bewitching pair of price and comfort.

But this is exactly what doesn't happen. Novelty tantalizes, ease and cheapness take us in their grip, and quality —the kind almost anyone can discern—is somewhat sheepishly replaced by variety. Only once this cultural shift of habits occurs, and the possibility of a return to previous ways appears impracticable, except on a niche scale, do we begin to wonder aloud whether something vital has been lost along the way. But even our wonder is marbled with cynicism; nostalgia is only a way of rendering the past unrecoverable, a place one visits with as much depth of feeling as a summer vacationer.

So it goes with much innovation, though hardly all. You couldn't regard the development of Wikipedia or Google Maps quite this way. And this is just because innovation is no more tied to regression than it is to progress. Which means we must ask, case by case, in perpetuity: What are the things in our lives *doing* there?

Distance Healing

The essential difficulty in migrating medical consultations online, right alongside everything else, is the loss of a physician's total powers of discrimination, which cannot be reduced to any set of discrete techniques or quantitative measures, as a computer's might. Diagnostic and therapeutic skill forms a gestalt, much as a patient's health does. Even if we could disseminate medical technologies widely so that every home was equipped with inexpensive and accurate measuring tools (blood pressure machines, swab kits), face-to-face examination gives physicians full access to evidence of pathology the patient himself may well overlook or otherwise fail to report, thinking it irrelevant to his complaint. Odd details—blotchy skin, twitching eyelids, bad breath—can be thick with meaning, given the sea of symptoms diseases may present. The capacity to notice, to judge significance, is a product of long training and apprenticeship; it cannot be left to the patient, as so many things are in an economy that leans ever more toward self-service.

The case of psychiatry, and the push in some quarters toward online sessions, is perhaps the clearest (though hardly the only) case of the shortcomings of virtual appointments. The intimacy and focus induced by physical proximity cannot be replicated onscreen, and it is just this closeness of observation, and the less codifiable evidence it yields—the slightest hesitation in response, the smallest break in a voice—that can be vital to successful diagnosis and therapy. These intangibles, this *feel* for the patient, are in various ways relevant to every medical consultation, psychiatric or not, and they are without doubt compromised by digital mediation.

Some will be tempted to shrug at this. After all, aren't human relations now quite generally degraded in this way? But this ignores the fact that the stakes are usually much lower, or less urgent, anyway. In the medical domain, where matters could not be more grave, the default lamentations over the loss of closeness between people in the modern world, usually proffered via those same technologies of alienation—Twitter, Zoom—isn't merely ironic and pathetic. It can be fatal. If we are incapable of resisting the siren song of ease in the rest of our lives, surely here—if our claim to valuing life *as such* is at all sincere—we must hold the line.

SPORTS

Ethical Athletics

Are players of violent sports like boxing, football, and ice hockey free actors? Does the justice of our watching them concuss each other wait on the answer?

Professional boxing traditionally draws its pugilists from the economic and social margins, where little reasonably compensated labor exists. Most fighters endure childhood poverty and violence; many have the rap sheets to show for it. Boxing saves troubled souls, they say, purging rage and offering redemption of a kind, if at a price. It's an *opportunity*, something in the fighters' interests, not a fate foisted on them by circumstance.

This isn't wrong, exactly. Boxing is a choice in a way that being dragged away to prison is not. Yet whenever I watch boxing, I find myself wondering, as the two men, bleary-eyed and slack-jawed, wobble onto their stools, their cornermen giving instructions they barely register, whether the choice to box is free *enough* to absolve me of the assistance I provide, through my spectatorship, in making the psychic and physical torment they experience in the ring profitable, especially given the greater suffering to come in retirement for those who carry on long careers: the memory lapses, the slurring, the jarring shifts of mood—the undoing of their selves, ultimately. And nothing at all feels as though it can make the pleasure I get from their punches innocent.

There are competitive endeavors—I hesitate to call them sports—even less voluntary than boxing: fighting dogs don't have any choice at all. That is why it's so easy to grasp what is morally dubious about it. Yet many boxers—and other athletes from hard-luck backgrounds—are separated only by degrees from this situation. Granted, they have declined *some* other economic opportunities, however mean, to box. But those jobs are frequently so poorly paid, insecure, and dangerous in their own ways, and the community infrastructure so weak, that no one would undertake them except out of direst necessity. A career in sports, however violent, would be a step up to anyone with the requisite physical talents: there are the potential riches, of course, but also the chance to embody courage, grace, and beauty. For such persons, there is no serious choice between these two paths; the undertaking is more necessary than voluntary. But if that is so, it makes little sense to suggest that most professional boxers have much of a say in picking their line of work. To take pleasure in their brutalization is to revel in the suffering of the innocent.

There are many other players for whom contact sports is no lifeline, merely a form of amateur recreation or, if it does become a career, a childhood dream come true. Given American football's evolution in the service academies and the Ivy League, and rugby's roots in Rugby School in England, we can assume that most who played for these schools or went on from there to play professionally didn't *need* to in any meaningful sense. For this reason, the Harvard-Yale game makes for less dubious viewing than most prize fights.

In either case, the question remains whether facilitating or taking pleasure in events that neurologically diminish athletes is a wrong of its own. For the mere fact that someone freely chooses to harm himself cannot morally cleanse my aiding his cause or enjoying its fulfillment.

Probably there are circumstances in which I *would* be blameless for doing so, even virtuous; certain cases of assisted suicide for the terminally ill come to mind. Yet one would think sponsoring activities that bring serious harm to others must in general carry a negative ethical valence.

The Sport in E-Sports

It's been years since ESPN started covering e-sports, yet the reluctance to admit video gaming into the pantheon of athletic competition persists. Its long associations with adolescent idleness have hurt it. The picture of teenagers pounding Mountain Dew and mashing buttons into the small hours instead of reading books or tossing *actual* balls around outdoors has proved indelible, even as demographics around gaming have evolved. There are other games one plays sitting down that don't share in this disrepute: chess, for instance, which ESPN also covers. There is less worry about its sporting status, even if it still seems misdescribed as such given the lack of athleticism involved. Yet the fabled pastime doesn't appear to require any legitimization: chess players don't much care whether you reckon them athletes; most think their form of intellectual competition is actually purer than mere sport. The game's complexity and austerity, not to mention the ancient tradition from which it springs, all serve to insulate it from accusations of frivolity. Competitive gaming cannot but seem juvenile in comparison; lives dedicated to conquering *Call of Duty* or *Fortnite* will always feel like lives misspent. This alone bars gamers from the realm of sport. A life given over to mastering one's body strikes us as noble in its way; nothing similar can be said about mastering a playable character.

That chess represents the disciplining of the mind, not the body, explains why it feels odd to call it a sport, no matter how much we esteem the game. At best it is a marginal case. Physical prowess and sports are conceptually linked. There are, of course, grossly out-of-shape sportsmen: the rotund middle-innings pitcher, the 350-pound defensive lineman who appears always on the brink of heart failure. Yet do they not excel in their assigned tasks, within the division of labor of their team? So they are sportsmen after all. That we may doubt the applicability of the concept of the athlete or sportsman to any person not having superior all-around physical capacities only recapitulates the tie between sports and the disciplining of the flesh.

Sports' Import

Professional sports demonstrate how a grown man running with a ball—or throwing, catching, or striking one—can be taken for a lodestar. Often in postgame press conferences or on-field interviews, the athlete, or even his coach, shows himself a bromidic savant, weaving tautologies and non sequiturs together. He knows not what he speaks, but speaks it confidently all the same. After all, *his* job isn't to digest this word salad—"let the big dog eat," "that's why we play the games," and, immortally, "they are who we thought they were"—only to offer it to reporters and fans with a taste for it.

Journalists bear equal responsibility for this ritualized postgame gibberish, a secular speaking in tongues. What else can players be expected to offer, half a minute or half an hour after the game, with their knees wrapped in ice, to queries like "What did it take to win this game?" A question this ill-formed is almost defiant in its triviality, daring the athlete to say something even more pointless. A classic reply? "Execution." Meaning the execution of the team's game plan. Meaning we won by doing what we planned on doing. Meaning we won because we won.

Still, isn't the familiar hollowness of this answer just the coda to the sporting drama we require? Once in a while, an athlete comes along with something substantive to say—real strategic insights, frank locker-room truths, or perspective-shifting gems about extra-athletic reality. Yet on the heels of a game, such intelligence is almost unwelcome, demanding more attention than our pleasant state of exhaustion allows. What we relish after three hours cheering on men regressing ever further into childhood is more pretense, more play: words that are not words, like the inflected mumblings heard through a common wall.

Even momentary contemplation shows that sports speak, properly done, can only ever be a nullity. The appeal this negation holds for the millions of people who've found white-collar success is curious and undeniable: *if only I, too, could have run with a ball right into adulthood (if not all the way to the grave), I would gladly have given my wits away.* I have heard even distinguished academics confess that they would have tossed all their books from the window for one chance to call Old Trafford or Fenway Park home. There is no one who dreams of deserting the mind for the innocent perfections of the body so acutely as the intellectual.

LANGUAGES

Concrete Thinking

The parable is sometimes derided as the most artificial of narrative forms, scrubbing away the motley accretion of detail to be found in documentary forms of imitation (*mimesis*). Yet spare, morally illustrative tales mimic real-life storytelling far better than more oblique accountings of events, which lack the clear practical import—the *point*—that, outside of expressly aesthetic contexts, makes lending one's ears a sensible proposition.

Parables merely refine the anecdotes we offer each other every day in conversation. Someone asks our advice on a decision they need to make: moving to a new country, taking a new job, getting married. How often do we begin to offer our wisdom thus: *Well, my friend moved to Shanghai . . .; A former colleague of mine left for a company like that . . .; My cousin actually married his high school sweetheart . . .*

As forms of reasoning go, anecdotes and their more refined cousins are elemental. It is no accident that most of the world's religious traditions are conveyed through them, and that philosophers since Plato have often grounded their ideas in them, too. This is thinking via story rather than theory, and it is far and away the most pervasive form, then and now.

The morals of parables are often accused of patness,

reducing the complexity of the world to truisms. Yet the more we examine them, whether the Garden of Eden, Billy Budd, or something altogether less artful, the more meaning we tend to find. Unlike a neatly stated theory, or even an allegory, which cuts its story to fit ideas already in hand, a great parable is a vast quarry of sense. Through its particular relation of characters and events, the authentic parable gestures at where veins of significance run, while leaving the audience to conduct the extraction for itself.

Lesser parables—they aren't worth the name, really—can fall into allegory, of course, just as fables like Aesop's do. Yet even these wooden tales pull their insights from the mines of anecdote and parable—the living embodiment of our wisdom.

Literature and the Lamp

That literary studies have given way to cultural studies over the past half-century, that the artistic value of a text is largely reckoned to be diagnostic vis-à-vis social ills, can only be put down to a pervasive worry about literature's import in the modern world, particularly the sort that finds little favor with the culture at large and so cannot sustain itself through market forces.

The line of thought runs thus: if unpopular art forms, and the study of such arts, are not to come across as mere aesthetic indulgences, other purposes must be found to vindicate them. Luckily, one lies at hand. Outside of the natural sciences, most areas of university life—and the university is far and away the great patron of the arts today—legitimize their activity on social grounds, in particular, the grounds of social justice. In MFA programs, poets and novelists are taught formal techniques for throwing disinfecting sunlight onto every benighted corner of life; in literature departments, scholars scour the poems and novels themselves for symptoms of social disease. The unstated aim, issuing from the university mission to produce knowledge for social improvement, is fostering a more just world.

One *might* have thought an abiding value of literature

and the other arts was the affordance of intrinsically valuable experiences, just as knowledge for its own sake is the defining aim of the basic sciences. Yet consensus on the worth and validity of scientific results is easier to come by than any similar agreement in the arts, where the problem of taste has loomed for over three centuries. The surest way of reaching accord on questions of artistic value is by sidestepping knotty philosophical debates and focusing on how artworks help us defend *other* values already avowed by the academy: equality, cultural diversity, inclusivity, and freedom. Understood as sources of knowledge about these ideals and their realization, literature and its study can only be seen as goods. The problem of taste falls away as irrelevant and the dangers of disengaged aesthetic experience are neatly met.

But assimilating literature and art to straightforwardly intellectual endeavors, turning them into knowledge-seeking discourses like the rest, fails to acknowledge that art is rarely compelling for its assertions. We don't come to, and anyway don't stay with, literature for the arguments. It's why the notion of paraphrasing a poem or a painting—unlike a line of reasoning—hardly makes sense to us.

This is one way of recovering something from the maligned notion of art's ineffability. There is something rationally ungovernable about it, something which puts it out of phase with every cognitive enterprise that can be instrumentalized at will. Simply *attending* to a novel or a poem, just as we might to a person, may be all that needs doing; our ideal response, the most difficult one, might be silence itself.

Lip Service

Conservative charges that certain acts are merely symptoms of social posturing or political correctness don't do much to limit public dialogue or the political imagination, as such aspersions are easily shown to instance the genetic fallacy: to deride white support for Black Lives Matter as kowtowing to ideological fashion can't preclude the substantive claims of advocates from receiving a hearing (from those prepared to listen, anyway). But when such derision is apt—when the truckling is real and widespread —real intellectual damage can be done.

Lip service widely paid thwarts exploratory speech. Whenever a proposition surfaces in the mind but the prospect of accurately translating it into the accepted terminology (supposing this even to be possible) appears onerous, the temptation arises to adopt easier but inferior tacks, like adverting to purposely vague language that lamely hints at the fugitive notion. As for the political imagination, approved speech erects not just social but psychological barriers to fertile thought in the social domain. Running afoul of widely avowed political sentiments—failing to genuflect before liberty, equality, or diversity as unconditional virtues, say—can create enough psychic pressure to push contrary thoughts under the rubric of absurdity, if not extrude them from the mind altogether.

Inner Dialogue

Experience and reason are usually contraposed. But what is the experience of thinking itself? Occasionally introspection reveals no debate at all, only a steady monologue, when the mind, sure of itself for the moment, proceeds in synchrony. A harried state, curiously, can also produce a single line of thought, when there's no time to indulge in any back and forth; one sticks close to the essential idea, sometimes a simple incantation to oneself, to carry one through distress. There are times, too, when we are so deeply engaged with the world that the inward aspect of the mind vanishes altogether from consciousness, and all thinking seems to be shunted into intelligent action, whether in athletics or painting or masonry.

Just as often, the voice in one's head multiplies instead of disappears. There is silent conversation, of course, but there's something just short of that we can consider first: two lines of thought unfurling at once, though any exchange between the two is limited at best. The experience of guilt, and of weakness of will, sometimes takes this form. *Nothing would be more foolish than doing that*, one thinks, just as the rest of one's mind is methodically working out how to do it.

Genuine inner dialogue is something different; it is the

height of human cognition. When we go about making hard choices, and we find no interlocuter worth consulting, we are forced to turn to our selves. Often one voice plays devil's advocate, doing all it can to undermine the logic of the other, though with the best of intentions: to bring about a more solid argument, a sounder course of action. There are times, though, when the self-quarreling is to no higher purpose, when it turns compulsive and paralyzing —Beckettian.

For the more cerebral, there can appear a third voice, one effectively calling the match between the other two. Indeed, some of us are able to follow the regress of voices quite a distance before losing track of who is saying what to whom.

The Language of Experience

Of dramatic experiences we say, "Words can't do it justice" or "It's indescribable." What could this mean? Words can represent almost anything that might happen to us. What they can't do is *replicate* experiences, and this is so whether they are extraordinary or banal. Compare eating strawberry ice cream with its description, even one worthy of Nabokov. Neither can substitute for the other, though the description can certainly elucidate its counterpart.

The upshot is that no experience can be put into words, save certain perceptual uses of *this* or *that* in which we literally point out the experienced thing we mean to our interlocutor: *Do you see that?* (But how much of the experience is in the *that*, so to speak, rather than in the world?) Language is not a vehicle of experience, delivering it to us whole as the post does a package.

The same holds for memory and the imagination. If I recall an encounter with my bodega cashier, or imagine him on another occasion, I don't somehow furnish myself with a current experience of either the cashier or the encounter. I merely represent them to myself, either at my whim (imagination) or in ways that causally trace to the prior event (memory).

That language fails to capture experience is no cause for

disappointment, as it isn't in the business of doing any such thing. If we can manufacture a linguistic representation of an experience, one that gives an idea of it without presuming to go proxy for it, then it has done its work. If more is wanted, if representation won't suffice for the purposes at hand, well, you're going to have to be there.

Bad Curses

What is most troubling about curse words is not their offensiveness but the way they shrink our descriptive powers when they take root in our lexicon. Although we do reach for the exotic one here and there, most of our swearing is done with just a small cluster of words (you know the ones). Maybe they number a dozen or two. Those who frequently use these all-purpose words are leaning heavily on a few blue concepts to do a great deal of descriptive work, homogenizing their speech. The effect, is anything *but* colorful.

A more careful use of expletives needn't create monotony. But isn't there always something malignant about them? They have the odd habit of chasing the finer words out of our vocabularies. Sparing use can quickly metamorphose into abuse. And as your comfort increases with them —and they *are* uncommonly comfortable, being the sweatpants of the language—the less precisely you find yourself speaking. This in turn induces a haziness of mind, of attention itself. When you become inured to crude expression, the world's terrific variety shrinks.

None of this casts doubt on the rhetorical power of obscenity, appropriately dispensed. A few well-chosen vulgarities can perfectly season your speech. So, if the occasion cries out for it, by all means, do swear. Just don't make a habit of it.

Writing and Thinking

Orwell was wrong: you *can* think profoundly and write dismally. Kant is not half the writer Nietzsche is, yet he must be twice the philosopher. I would go further. At least sometimes, tortuous prose is the ineradicable symptom of thinking at the very edge of what is intelligible, a territory elegance rarely visits.

Conversely, too great an ease with language can lead to glibness and a kind of scattering of light. Nietzsche is innocent on this score; his fluency only deepened his thinking. Less sure is the case of Isaiah Berlin, who often fell under the spell of his own phrasemaking, in conversation and in writing. A bit less verve might have slowed him down just enough to let him burrow deeper, instead of airily flitting about.

One fears even more for Berlin's acolytes, like the brilliant blowhard Leon Wieseltier, or Christopher Hitchens, purveyor of a singularly louche bombast. An effortless way with words assured their journalistic triumph as certainly as it did Orwell's. It also alienated them all from the farthest reaches of thought.

CHARACTERS

Respectable Prejudice

It can be hard to resist seeing moral improvement, and political progress, as achieved largely through the patient rooting out of bias—prejudice, in one way of speaking—from our thoughts and deeds. But there are risks in acquiescence.

Taken to the limit, the drive toward ever greater impartiality can make nihilists of us. The very idea of ethics, of having normative reasons for action generally, depends on the notion that some arrangements of the universe are, in some sense or other, to some*one* or other, better than others. Might a truly unbiased view of the world, though, favor no particular state of affairs over any other? This seems like a recipe for agential paralysis. How, after all, are we to decide how to act in a world lacking any moral tilt? We might do better, it seems, to give a regulative role to impartiality *within* our moral framework rather than expect it to serve as a foundation for an entire ethic. This would be to be partial toward impartiality, to wit, to hold that the preeminent moral and political norms are indifferent to many of the empirical differences between agents. As Rawls did with his veil of ignorance, we would then have license to peel away the specifics of our lives—our ancestry, race, sexuality, economic status, religion, even our geographic location—in deciding on how best to arrange society's basic structures. The guiding thought would be that these differences are irrelevant from the moral point of view. Need they be, though? Rawls originally held that any rational agent should be able to see the moral legitimacy of his veil, that is, of his deployment of impartiality in ethics, and therefore in the political principles that would issue from it, which are tantamount to welfare-state liberalism. He turned modest with age, claiming his theory of justice only codified some core *intuitions* prevalent in certain Western societies. Critics, of course, might well call these prejudices.

Even in the West, though, our intuitions are hardly uniform. For advocates of impartialist ethics, the money I once donated to a soup kitchen in New York would have gone further, and *done more good*, as we say, in Detroit or Memphis, or indeed, on even more strongly impartialist views—ones that disregard national boundaries, like Peter Singer's utilitarianism—in Calcutta or Lagos, where they would have done *much* more good, given the strength of the dollar. My own feeling is that there is more to ethics than the general reduction of suffering in the world or even just the state. Assisting those whose lives are closely woven with my own, who walk the same streets, sit in the same parks, and ride the same subways, seems to me to take precedence over helping mere strangers, whether they lie across the country or the world. With family and close friends, of course, the interdependency relations are all the more robust, and this is so wherever they may be scattered geographically. Here our moral obligation to aid them becomes stronger still, even if one's resources manifestly do less good in mitigating human suffering, impartially speaking.

Such moral tiering falls under the maxim of taking care of one's own, where *one's own* is defined by just this inter-wovenness, the intimate sharing of lives and ways of life—and not by anything so simple as nationality, gender, geography, or race. Such closeness cannot exist among people who have neither experienced much together nor expect to in the future, although there is no point at which the weave comes apart entirely: global phenomena like climate change and the international markets bind all of us together.

Yet to the extent I am partial toward those whose lives are more tightly entwined with mine, I can be said to bear prejudice against those with weaker ties: they count for less to me—and generally I to them. This is no bad thing. Communities with personality, the kinds we all want to be a part of, depend partly on the existence of just these sorts of biases, as Burke suggested long ago. Neutrality dulls the spirit.

Honest Performances

There are at least two levels of performance: the kind we call second nature, and the kind that's conscious and deliberate. Whatever becomes second nature to us, though residing in consciousness through the initial learning stages, transforms through repetition into instinct. Once we have mastered the parts, we play our various roles, whether of cousin, vegan, soldier, or more general ones like man, woman, or citizen, without premeditation. That such inhabitation nevertheless qualifies as a kind of performance can be freeing; it suggests we might rewrite our parts, form new habits, and ultimately open the way to new forms of being.

While some flexibility of identity is doubtless to the good, what of someone who seems to try on new identities like coats, carrying the manner of adolescence well into adulthood? You find him a different person every few years: a sculptor just out of college, a corporate lawyer when things go south, a non-profit worker since the guilt set in, and the last time you checked, he'd gone off the grid with hardly an explanation.

Flexibility has turned into formlessness, and the full development of human character, which requires confronting durable constraints, is stunted by this incessant shuffling of roles. To refuse to accept limits, even provisional limits, on what one is, leaves one vulnerable to ending up nothing in particular, just a collection of shallow performances never carried to perfection. Such dilettantes of the soul shift gears before the world can offer real resistance to their aims, so they remain much as dabblers do in the arts: amateurs, yet in a far more tragic sense.

This is the risk of seeing life as a performance: insouciance can replace conviction and commitment; the story of one's life can overtake the living itself. Yet the basic insight, that what appears natural or essential to us may not be, can be put to good use if we can refrain from casually swapping out the basic shape of our life and instead put most of our energies toward exploring, and indeed expanding, the roles we occupy. Coming to see our ways of being as unconsciously performed, and hence our identities as malleable, can help in this.

Virtually Authentic

It is tempting to think the far-reaching potential for anonymity online makes the internet a place of greater authenticity than the ordinary world. After all, being unidentifiable does let you speak more freely and involve yourself more widely without fear. But it is easy to over-state how much time we actually spend online with our identities cloaked.

In the early days of the internet, anonymous browsing, chatting, and commenting made up the lion's share of our activity. Today, much of our online commerce is conducted under our own names, whether through social media or the avatars of the various organizations our lives are built around: schools, recreational groups, governmental and financial institutions. And the most notable quality of the online version of ourselves is entirely at odds with authenticity or naturalness: the capacity to endlessly curate our self-presentation, controlling the story we put across to others in ways that are not possible in the flesh.

Certain features of the internet give us reasons to sculpt ourselves in these ways. To start with, much online material is accessible by anyone at any time, for as long as the servers live. Ordinary social intercourse is ephemeral, having no life beyond the actual time spent in another's company, so it is only natural that we will exercise a greater degree of circumspection in how we present ourselves in cyberspace as compared with real life.

There is also the general social expectation that forms of communication not involving extemporaneity—most writing and online interaction—are held to higher standards. What in a spoken exchange we might overlook as a slip of the tongue, an infelicitous phrase, or a raw formulation, we often won't excuse in premeditated communication. It is the presumed deliberateness of writing that gives it a special authority—one we would rather it didn't have sometimes. This is why we must closely manage whatever appears under our own names, much of which is now online.

Some of this self-editing is perfectly deliberate and well scaled to the relative importance of what we are saying; yet after a time, this reflexivity cannot but seep into our digital demeanor, lending everything we do a peculiar stagey quality. This is the very tenor of the internet itself.

A final reason our cyberencounters can be so stilted: simple decontextualization. In writing and other forms of online communication, words, images, and sounds are forced to carry the entirety of our meaning, without the benefit of the environmental cues (body language, indexical expressions) that fill in and delimit just what we mean to say when we speak. A greater explicitness is therefore required online to avoid misunderstandings. Yet this necessity can end up obscuring our most natural, unselfconscious intent—which is precisely what we seek sometimes. Disembodied intercourse gives us the chance to cherry-pick our sentiments and offer up a carefully composed picture of who we are or what we think, in a way the impromptu vagaries of in-the-flesh conversation threaten to undermine. It is just this threat, of course, that makes the couch valuable to the psychiatrist, the job interview to a hiring committee, and the park bench to almost anyone. There is a kind of opportunity for knowledge here that goes missing online.

But *which* is our most authentic self? The least or most manicured? We tend to assume it's the former, equating rawness with reality. But why should that be? Perhaps our most considered self represents us most richly, in which case the very deliberateness of online life might bring into view who we are in a way real life cannot.

More likely, the perfectly assembled self, no less than the unmediated version, fails to deliver what is really wanted, which is the most *revealing* picture of who we are. That requires an admixture of frankness *and* fastidiousness: in short, an honest performance. And this bit of alchemy is still most reliably effected the old-fashioned way, by looking someone in the eyes.

Unknown Pleasures

Anonymity emboldens. The difficulty is that we cannot know in advance whether this forwardness will harm more than help us. Incognito, we are free to indulge our worst selves, venting our feelings unchecked, declaiming our least reasonable thoughts, reveling in the instinctive satisfactions of bigotry without repercussion. Can anyone know themselves so well as to rule out the possibility that shielding his identity *won't* draw out something perverse in him?

We might well forswear anonymity if all it did was corrupt character. But the good that anonymity can do the spirit is profound, even the spirit of someone it has shown to be deficient in just this respect. It can cure the very defects of character it reveals by making it easier to flirt with otherness, to peer into alternative subcultures, to confront difference, all of which our public personae often cannot bear without our appearing uncertain, incoherent, or hypocritical. Negative capability is easier to exercise in private; without fear of disgrace, the liminal space between ideas, between selves, becomes permeable, so that even those who seek anonymity only to veil their ugliest desires can find themselves, through the unguarded (because

unseen) exposure to the variousness of humanity, relieved
of those drives.

FEELINGS

The Heart

There are at least two ways of thinking about *the heart*. First, there are the ungrounded preferences we have for some things over others. The heart here signifies the inscrutable nature of desire, which may pull against everything rational or ethical; it is then that we invoke the contrast between reasonable thoughts and unreasonable feelings.

But the heart also manages to signify the opposite, something once called the moral sense. We are still firmly in the realm of feeling, but now of a different order. This is the heart not as the antagonist of reason, something alien to it to be worked around like an obstacle, but feeling as the affective emissary of practical reason, to be consulted just when one is besieged by fancy: "Would acting on these passions clash with what I truly feel in my heart?" Far from representing something capricious, the heart is a repository of wisdom, but in the form of feeling, not thought.

Whenever we seek advice, we are so frequently told, in one way or another, to trust our heart, to follow it, consult it. The ubiquity of this reply derives from its double meaning. Are we to trust our unpredictable feelings rather than relying on reason and deliberation? Or are we to consider our principled feelings, as it were, to see if they comport with the decision we are tempted to make? Following your heart can mean either of these things, and frequently this is just the way our confidantes would have it. Take it as you will.

Judging by Feelings

I doubt that our emotional responses to the world intrinsically guide us toward ethical truth; but the circumstances that induce particular feelings in a person, as Aristotle held, tell us much about his character, so that they can help us distinguish right-minded people from the rest.

Someone may know there is nothing wrong with homosexual relationships. Yet the sight of men kissing still disgusts him. This is an affective response *not* befitting the circumstance, and this follows simply from what it means for homosexuality to be morally acceptable. Hence his disgust here indicates a flaw in his character. Worse still, his feelings don't even square with his beliefs about the matter, since he himself accepts the permissibility of same-sex relationships. It shows his mind to be in conflict with itself, not just the world.

Emotional reactions have no *intrinsic* validity to them. As with beliefs, the appropriateness of affective states depends upon prevailing environmental conditions. Just as it is part of ordinary cognitive development that we come to reliably form true perceptual beliefs about the world around us—we tend to believe we're looking at the moon only when we *are* in fact looking at the moon—moral maturation involves our developing emotional responses that fit the situation at hand.

The failure to feel anything much under certain conditions can also demonstrate an ethical lack. You know that child molestation is a despicable thing; and yet suppose you feel no queasiness, disgust, or horror hearing such acts described on the evening news. Something in your emotional makeup is off. There are situations that *should* induce disgust in those with a developed moral sense.

Though emotional reactions may not function like a compass, steering us toward the right and the good, so long as we have an independent handle on those notions, they can reveal how affectively attuned someone is to our shared moral life, or even just to his own worldview. Our normative appraisal of others and even of ourselves, in moments of self-reflection, depends in part on these relationships.

Approaching Happiness

If happiness requires one or another means of pursuit, namely, the various tangible activities that bring you satisfaction—relationships, career achievements, travel, reading, opera, sports, or whatever—the abstract pursuit of happiness as such needn't interfere with the pleasures yielded by any of these ends. You pursue happiness just by pursuing any number of happy-making activities.

Sometimes it happens that we're wrong about what brings us satisfaction. You might come to believe a certain thing *ought* to please you—concert music, say—because it brings pleasure to people you admire. That's not a bad reason, really, to try to pick up the habit. Yet it's perfectly possible you'll find, after you've heard half the ensembles in town, attending shows with devotees, that the music fails to bring you joy. It is here, if you don't give it up, that the abstract pursuit of happiness will inhibit your opportunities for experiencing any, because you've made an empirical mistake about your sensibilities: the music just doesn't suit you. Perhaps you should stick to rock 'n' roll for happiness, and listen to symphonies, if you must, for edification. There is nothing, after all, in the concept of knowledge suggesting that happiness goes hand in hand with it.

Confidence and Arrogance

I can't remember the last time I described someone as arrogant, though I must be acquainted with as many lordly sorts as anyone else—they are not rare, really. It must be because I opt for other semicognate terms to characterize many of them: *deluded, foolish, lost.* For the balance, *confident* is my adjective of choice.

The use of one or the other modifier—*confident* or *arrogant*—tells you at least as much about the appraiser as the appraised. Those who fear error and the judgment of others tend to see hubris everywhere, and schadenfreude is their close companion when it comes to those they think arrogant. Bolder people, or simply the less self-conscious, tend not to find as much presumptuousness in the world; in its place there is simply confidence or, at the limit, audacity. They also revel less in the missteps of others—at least those stemming from assertiveness—as they don't see travails as fatal to the ultimate realization of ambition.

Arrogance *is* connected with some sense of exceptionalism or superiority, of course. The confident may take their chances, but they needn't feel they have special aptitudes that justify it, as the arrogant do. Sometimes they are just more willing to gamble, and may think that if others could only overcome their fear, they could have just the same chance at success.

When the arrogant do fail decisively, they are often unwilling to acknowledge this at all, choosing instead to blame someone else's deficiencies for the defeat. Whereas the confident needn't be defensive about even irredeemable failure, since nothing about bold action suggests ultimate victory. That seems to be arrogance's domain.

Still, isn't there something useful about arrogance, even if it's an unbecoming attitude to find in others and regularly trades in delusion? Believing you are destined ultimately to succeed can be a productive false belief for the one who holds it. You may doggedly persist in some endeavor, against all evidence, just because you have the false sense that your talents are too great for things to end in defeat. And precisely for that extra effort, conjured through sheer conceit, you may end up succeeding, where a more sensible person would have folded long ago.

Blissful Problems

The problem of groundless bliss is well captured by Robert Nozick's *experience machine*, which is more or less what a perfected virtual reality device would be like. Would it make for a good life, he wondered, to have such an instrument deliver a maximum of pleasurable experience—total bliss, however you rate it? An actual life, unmediated by the machine, will almost always generate less pleasure, often far less. Yet it seems clear that, as Nozick would have it, the latter kind of life is more worthwhile than the former, even though it is a less happy one. Pleasure, *pace* hedonism, cannot be the ultimate good. What matters is not just experience's qualitative character, but *what* one's experience is of: a simulation of reality, or the genuine article.

One theological consequence: experience of heaven, as Abrahamic religions conceive it, cannot be equivalent to the objectless experience provided by Nozick's machine, even if one can't subjectively distinguish between the two. Heavenly experience is, first, experience *of* a place, even if it isn't contiguous with ordinary space-time. The source of such pleasure is the contents of *heaven*, not the electrodes placed on the skull or images generated before the eyes. For an atheist, of course, there can be no distinct place called heaven. Hence the only kind of heavenly experience possible will be virtual. The bliss machine is the best we can do to satisfy the religious impulse, which will be no comfort to the devout.

Another formulation: what is it that troubles us about the so-called simulation hypothesis, the notion that we are all probably *already* living in a virtual reality, even if it's hardly all bliss? Surely that it is ersatz experience. Who can be entirely content with a replica if the real thing still exists?

Even so, if our familiar world were simulated through and through, we would have reason enough to carry on living just as we do now, with all the same normative concerns. So long as the experienced consequences of our simulated deeds remain unchanged, our reasons for action do, too. Which is to say, when *all* the world depends on features of our subjectivity, as it did for Kant, it might as well be real, for all that it matters to our lives. It is only when *parts* of our world are illusory, and other parts real—and we can tell one from the other to boot—that our practical lives register any difference: our phantasms, once revealed, earn from us only insouciance.

Resignation's Resurgence

Bastardized versions of Greek Stoicism and Zen Buddhism have come into fashion with technology entrepreneurs and other urban elites over the past half decade, and the timing makes good sense. The appeal of any philosophy of detachment surges in unruly eras, when the world seems so completely to resist our efforts to reform it. That is one way of seeing the matter: the preferred way, in fact. Climate change, the concentration of capital, ideological polarization, energy shortages, indiscriminate violence against innocents, radical populism—it is hard to feel anything but defeated by the scope of these issues. Yet it is equally difficult not to feel implicated in the mess, all the more so for the Silicon Valley businessmen who have starred in the dramatic crises of our moment. For an industry weaned on the vanities of utopianism and led by corporations with slogans like *Don't be evil*, assuaging guilt is a crucial mission. And there is no better way to do it, short of actually *not* being evil, than adopting a stance of quiet resignation toward the world's fate (as if they had no hand in it) and merely disciplining their emotional reactions rather than their destructive actions. In this way, they conveniently divorce their personal welfare—and they are faring very well, indeed—from the welfare of the world at large.

Stoicism and Buddhism both fit the bill in promoting attitudes of equanimity, come what may, and accepting suffering as inevitable. But they also counsel personally comporting oneself in an ethically defensible way, to wit, refraining, to the greatest extent possible, from adding to the miseries of the world. Here is where the shell games begin. We should not mistake the growing silence of businessmen on the redemptive powers of digital technology for a newfound, inward-looking spirituality. The utopianism, a quarter-century later, looks deluded or self-serving or both. *That* is the reason for the retreat into silence. Nor should we conflate the purely self-involving changes they make to their way of life—adopting meditation, rigorous outdoor activity, fasting—with the full range of change required by either philosophy. Other-involving changes—altering one's professional activities if they have damaging consequences for the wider world, for one—must also be made. But it is precisely these that they will not countenance, which leaves their philosophical commitments a farce.

ARTS

Satirical Significance

Gulliver's Travels, Tartuffe, and *Candide* remain valuable, even if we are far removed from the contemporary social controversies that gave these books a different sort of life in their own times. They have lost their original critical function, and much of their acerbity, and we shouldn't pretend this has no bearing on their artistic effect. What, then, are we appreciating in them when we enjoy them today?

Perhaps we are not appreciating them as satire per se, though it is not as if we fail to see how they deride their targets. Still, the mockery has lost its punch, as the issues at hand—the church, in *Tartuffe*—are either dead or barely recognizable these centuries later. You could call them embalmed satires.

Satires to which we are still fully alive, like George Saunders's short stories, have targets still too threatening for us to feel distant from, which naturally effects our manner of apprehension. These stories and all other "live" satires draw their power not just from the inherent qualities of the reading experience, substantial though they may be, but from a criticism that is aimed squarely at the reader's own world.

What exactly is the value of this blend? Satirical critique is less direct than the essayistic variety, which can lead to unclarity about both its stakes and solutions. Poor specimens devolve into ridicule, the sort that depoliticizes its audience by making the mere mockery of the world's corrupt ways satisfying in itself, without spurring any reform. But an exemplary satire can shift the center of gravity of a culture, however minutely, bringing action in its wake. Paul Beatty's *The Sellout* is satire of a pungent sort, concerning a man surreally trying to revive slavery in modern America. As violently angry as it is just beneath its comic surface, the novel went on to take the Booker Prize in 2015. There can be no doubt that this book, taken together with many other cultural forces gesturing in the same direction, managed to soften long-standing callousness toward black suffering in America and alter the felt burden of proof in broader debates about cultural power.

For future generations, of course, the book will be something different. Formal pleasures will endure while its edges dull, inasmuch as later audiences fall short, as they must, of a total empathetic projection into our early twenty-first-century lives.

The Religious Conception of Art

A sophisticated intellectual grasp of the symbolic content of religious art, the kind secular art historians very often have, is not inconsistent with being unequipped to feel their affective force. The situation is reminiscent of a famous thought experiment: imagine a scientist who knows all there is to know about the physics of color and yet is colorblind. In one sense, he understands color profoundly; in another, he has missed its experiential essence.

When we do not share the cultural frame of reference within which a given work of art emerges, there are bound to be features of it that fail to register with us. That doesn't mean an alien vantage has no use. It can bring to the fore artistic qualities that were obscure to the original viewers precisely for occupying the same *Lebenswelt*.

When a secular viewer today regards religious paintings from the Italian Renaissance, their formal properties—the radiance of the tempura, the delicacy of the brushwork—might well call attention to themselves in ways they didn't in their own time. His exclusion from the cultural horizon upon which the painting first appeared, though barring entry to certain spiritual depths of the work, reveals other aspects for appraisal.

It is not just to the formal aspects of artworks that this applies. New significances also come into view, sometimes no less profound than the originals'. You may, for instance, look upon the epic premodern depictions of Jesus as the son of God not with the hushed reverence of long-dead audiences, but with a fresh, this-worldly pathos unavailable to them and perhaps no less poignant for it: Jesus as an ordinary man, whose single-minded commitment to a redemptive cause recast the world.

Cultural distance precludes certain forms of understanding just as it opens the way to new ones.

The Life or the Work, II:
David Foster Wallace

Emerson's 1850 collection *Representative Men* explicates a series of archetypes through certain historical incarnations: Goethe was the Writer, Napoleon the Man of the World, and Montaigne the Skeptic. David Foster Wallace can be added to this group, though only by means of a far less grand kind, one who is, however, dearer to the heart of his times (the early 1990s): the Slacker. Overeducated, kultur-critical, prone to withering self-doubt and more-than-casual drug use, Wallace was, like so many of his generation, both contemptuous and desirous of status. He had many peers—Vollmann and Franzen, most notably—but by virtue of his outsize persona, he was better suited to trans-mutation into a cultural trope.

No doubt Wallace was a significant talent, but not for being a singular one. For disaffected litterateurs of a certain age, he was a representative man, capable of articulating their common predicament better than they could them-selves. This might have been inadvertent at first—although there are early signs of his grasping after the voice-of-a-generation mantle—but after his Kenyon commencement speech and a good part of his journalism had been produced, it is clear he deliberately sought the pundit's mantle more than the novelist's as such. This is why, ultimately, it is Wallace himself, *qua* embodiment of an emerging kind of cultural figure, more than his fiction (which he thought his highest achievement), that is responsible for the esteem in which he is held now, even if the work has inherited some of that luster, for proximal generations at least.

Like other figures in the arts—Louis CK, Quentin Tarantino, Karl Ove Knausgaard—Wallace did not simply deploy some preternatural gift for observation to capture contemporary culture as an outsider might. Rather, it was *he* who was captive to the culture—so much so that others could come to understand their own condition through reflecting on his work, which was more of an expression or symptom of the culture than a representation of it.

He did, it is true, have great powers of observation, as the cliché runs. He could resolve details many of his generation could not quite bring into focus, and that has made him a useful guide for all those caught in the phenomenological wake of Gen-X malaise. His writing fills out a worldview they grasp only in outline, or understand intuitively, and helps codify their collective feeling for the times.

What his works don't consistently do is explore unfamiliar ways of feeling about the world, and new frames of reference for grasping it. Whatever the formal novelty of his work, the sensibility conveyed thereby is pervasive among his demographic: young, learned liberals finding their place in an alienated world. Yet it is only by proffering a reorientation toward life that an artist or intellectual can genuinely shift the direction of our attention. *That* is how a writer discloses what has so far made no real impression on his culture, rather than merely clarifying what is already a hazy object of collective attention. Coetzee, Sebald, Naipaul, and Marías all succeeded in effecting these sorts of reorientations, enlarging our sense of life rather than simply sharpening up the one we've got. And they could only do so because they were *not* representative men.

The Origins of Artistic Talent

Often we use the word *talent* to mean *natural facility*. In this sense, there is little doubt talent varies in the realm of art. Siblings raised in the same household need not take equally to every art. One might draw more easily and naturally than the other, who for her part might have an easier time picking out melodies than making sketches. The particular notion of artistic talent in play here is a facility with *craft*, which we measure against a more or less objective standard, one of mimesis: the ability to precisely imitate some feature of reality, visual, aural, or whatever. When we say of someone, "He can't sing," we generally mean he has trouble reproducing pitches in rhythm, not that his rendition lacks charm or gravitas or some other more intangible quality. The same goes for attributing the talent for drawing or dancing.

These mimetic talents can, within limits, be honed, so that someone more naturally gifted as a singer or draftsman in the artisanal sense can be outdone by someone of lesser innate facility but with stronger training (in music theory or linear perspective, for two).

There is another conception of talent, though, on which someone who can sing perfectly well in the prior sense might not be able to sing at all. She may hit all the right notes, but the interpretation is lacking in expressive nuance, control, or verve. There are also those who embody the converse proposition. In the realm of the visual arts, the case of Saul Steinberg sheds light. His mimetic skills as a draftsman weren't truly elite; but his imaginative use of line was, by common consent, extraordinary and profound, so that one hardly cares about this lack of empirical accuracy. As with the artisanal sense of talent, the visionary sense may also be grounded in certain native capacities of the mind—a gift for association and metaphor, say. And this sort of ability may well be less replicable by hard graft than the former. Technical study needn't substantially improve one's creative powers in the way it can be counted on doing so in matters of craft. Certainly we know of no fixed regimen for the imagination that generates anything like the steady, measurable success of formal training in instilling the gifts nature has withheld.

Creative Austerity

The thing about creative drive, which you can just as well think of as a kind of pressure, is that there are so many ways it can be dissipated. Whenever I find that I'm not writing much of anything, or even just anything with real vigor to it, I usually discover—and always as if for the first time—that there are too many valves open, bleeding off this pressure. The releases are many, and some are unexpected. Food, for one. Curiously, I cannot write anything worthwhile on a full stomach. In fact, hunger itself may serve as a useful metaphor for thinking about creativity. A certain kind of intellectual and emotional deprivation can yield work of greater intensity. All sorts of pleasures, both worthy and trivial, can seem to blunt it: watching films, reading, browsing the web, socializing, romance, too much sleep even. So, to find my way back to my sharpest writing, Spartan self-denial is generally the answer. Which is to say, to come around to the earlier metaphor, the valves must be tightened and the pressure must build. Invariably, within a few days, I reach a state of productive agitation, restless to write again, to probe with words. Almost magically, a reassuring force is restored to my writing, to my mind.

Perennial Art

Art that seeks, in Goethe's phrase, the "characteristic" of the era, tends to be valued, in later epochs, more for the historical insight it provides than for the aesthetic experience it affords. Goethe's own novels, important as they are in understanding the history of the medium, as well as late eighteenth-century Europe, do not retain the verve of *Tristram Shandy*, *Gargantua and Pantagruel*, or *Don Quixote*, works which only incidentally deal in the representative or characteristic. Goethe may only have been following Aristotle, who suggested that poetry is nobler than history precisely for privileging the typical over the contingent. Yet an artwork's vitality, particularly for future generations, may have far more to do with properties like ambiguity, richness, and even outright contradiction than with cogent summations of a historical moment. It is why nineteenth-century novelists who emphasized the latter—Balzac and Zola—are more often cited than read today, whereas the works of the more enigmatic Melville and Conrad retain their original luster. Consider, too, the case of Goncharov, whose first novel signaled his intentions plainly through its title, *A Common Story*, and who is now much less read than his contemporary Dostoevsky, whose books, while remaining emblematic of Russian consciousness, tackle weightier matters: freedom, God, evil, and the rest. More recently, the fate of many an American social novelist has followed the same pattern. Why are we no longer entranced by Dreiser or Anderson, Dos Passos or Wilder, each of whom aimed to give an account of the essence of country, the spirit of the age? What, too, of later writers operating in a similar vein, whether Mailer or Vidal or Wolfe?

It feels inevitable that the first significant twenty-first-century addition to this list will be Jonathan Franzen. *The Corrections*, a fine précis of its moment, already feels as though it has lost some gravitas, while *Freedom* and *Purity* both felt dated upon their release.

John Updike also aspired to chronicle suburban America in broad strokes. News value put him, like Franzen, on the cover of *Time*. But interest in Updike's work *today* is already more aesthetic than informational. Style, concept, and vision are what survive in art, not the well-articulated facts of the moment. Updike had at least a version of the first: an effortless capacity for painterly description. It is *this*, and not his chronicle of post-war America, that keeps our attention, though I suspect his style is too conceptually banal to keep it for much longer. He is already on his way out.

Franzen has even bigger worries, being overmatched by Updike as a stylist. In his *Paris Review* interview, Franzen dismisses style, praising transparent language. Quiet prose isn't the problem, though: the radically expansive realism of *War and Peace*—which contains whole essays on the philosophy of history—is put across entirely in it. It is only because the *substance* of Franzen's project is so much humbler than Tolstoy's that stolid language rates as a liability.

The reaction to much of Franzen's recent journalism for the *New Yorker* is instructive. His long features on both bird conservation and the two-degree global warming target have both been roundly derided as shrill, misinformed, and

dogmatic. His fiction is less marred by righteous indignation, but not by much, at least since *The Corrections*. That
book inaugurated Franzen's Dreiser period. And if literature is the news that stays news, as the old saw goes, this
work isn't quite it.

There remains Franzen's early period, which yielded
two heady novels at some remove from the social chroni-
cles that followed. Though *The Twenty-Seventh City* and
Strong Motion are now hardly discussed, there are reasons
to think they will become his most enduring contributions
to literature.

One wonders, too, which of the novels of the decade
just past will soon be regarded as period pieces. The
fashion during this stretch for diary fiction—true journalism, if ever there were—suggests that the most widely
discussed works of the 2010s will have more than a little
trouble sticking in the mind.

To Collect and to Hoard

Collecting is a child's pursuit. When the young gather rocks or cards or dolls, we are warmed by the activity's familiarity. When adults do the same—I mean collect for its own sake, not as a means of investment—our curiosity cannot be but piqued. For the adult collector is necessarily quirky, driven by a charmingly unreasonable attachment to a whole class of objects, whatever the class, that is usually only indulged in one's early youth.

We are in the territory of obsession here, but its more enchanted reaches: a state of prolonged and gentle infatuation, which is the natural tenor of childhood itself.

Collecting should never be mistaken for mere acquisition, the simple accumulation of objects of some type over time. Rather, it is an enterprise fueled by purposeful engagement. Looking in my closet, I see many pairs of loafers, perhaps significantly more than average. That hardly makes me a collector. Mindful selection and serial acquisition are worlds apart.

This suffices to distinguish collecting from hoarding. When, on one of those television programs that make entertainment out of pathology, one sees a house overflowing with bedraggled newspapers indiscriminately piled into drifts that threaten to sweep the hoarder himself away, the word *collector* is far from the tip of one's tongue. Missing from the hoarder's sensibility is the curatorial instinct of the collector, including any drive to preserve or honor the gathered objects. It is only a curious inability to dispose of things, even things paid hardly any attention, rather than any positive desire to collect, that defines the hoarder.

Collectors, however odd we may find them, inspire a degree of admiration in us, not least because they, like artists, have kept a channel open to childhood and its unprofitable concerns rather than allowing themselves to be chastened by adulthood into a hard-headed pragmatism. There is, by contrast, nothing much to envy in hoarders.

Unread Books

Books are now published in numbers so vast that the writing of one can no longer be presumed to be an act of communication. Yet volumes unread, or even unpublished, can have their value.

Unbound prose offers the writer a chance, one never to be encountered in conversation, no matter how patient her listeners, to comb slowly through her own mind, sorting out her thoughts and reflexively exploring her sensibilities. Along the way, catharsis too may be in the offing; any troubling feelings discovered while writing may be discharged —if she can only figure out how—without needing to involve readers in the least.

It is a pleasurable challenge simply to write at great length, not to appreciate one's own voice but to carry off a sustained fluency ordinary life never asks of us. There is also something to be said, in publishing a book, for putting oneself in a position to be read, even if that reading remains notional for some or all time. Creating a potential communicative act, even if one knows not when, where, or with whom it may be fulfilled, gestures at the fundament of expression.

Deep Thoughts

Academic specialization depends upon taking large tracts of collateral knowledge for granted and, building from those assumptions, working out a narrow set of conclusions. This sort of voluntary blinkering, not so different from the way factories break down manufacturing processes previously united in the guilds they replaced, risks obscuring the very point of the broader endeavor— the original aims animating the field—from the workers themselves. This is, in Kuhnian terms, a difficulty inherent in what he calls normal science, in which the underlying conceptual framework structuring the discipline doesn't come in for much scrutiny.

In analytic philosophy, for instance, there are so-called formal epistemologists who spend their days painstakingly working out logical models of our communal use of the concept of knowledge, with the goal of trying to capture as many of the ordinary inferences we are inclined to make involving the word *know*, while disallowing all the inferences we are not inclined to make. The problem is then further subdivided: the problem of knowledge and subjunctive conditionals; the problem of knowledge and the future tense; and so on.

Academic philosophers of this stripe, who often can

offer terrifically detailed models of our inferential practices, have oddly impoverished answers to questions of this stripe: What is the significance of logical inference in the explication of knowledge? What are our grounds for thinking that our commonsense epistemic inferences are correct, that we know the things we pretheoretically think we do? Ever since the time of Socrates, hasn't assessing the plausibility of commonsense ideas been one of the central concerns of epistemology and of philosophy more generally?

Typically, all you'll draw with this line of inquiry are long stares, as these questions, seemingly the very heart of epistemology, are not ones to which attention is given in their particular subspecialty. If anything, these big-picture issues surrounding knowledge are only seen as a distraction from working out detailed models of inference.

Yet many of the breakthroughs in these subspecialties require the work of thinkers who stay permanently alive to the classical philosophical questions, however much trouble those questions make for the particulars of their theories. The English philosopher Michael Dummett's constructivist arguments about linguistic meaning, drawn from foundational regions of the philosophy of mathematics, had a profound effect on resensitizing rank-and-file philosophers of language and logic to the possibility that some of our inferential practices, including those surrounding our claims to knowledge, might be in need of revision, involving as they do, Dummett thought, a defective conception of truth as potentially evidence-transcendent.

Beyond carving out an alternative approach to logic and epistemology, Dummett's critique of philosophical orthodoxy drove other thinkers, like Donald Davidson, to find better ways of defending that very notion of truth, in just the way that the epistemological problems posed by Hume motivated Kant to offer his transcendental philosophy. Dummett and Davidson, Hume and Kant, could only achieve what they did, though, by keeping in mind the deep, ancient questions of knowledge that give philosophy its point while simultaneously surveying the minutia on the forefronts of the field as they found it in their times.

There is nothing at all easy in seeing the forest *and* the trees. But it is what the most fertile thinkers manage, and so it ought to be our aim at least.

MONIES

Free Form

Every art relates to commerce in its own way, but for those in which the cost of entry is low—painting, literature—it is routine for watershed works to emerge without the benefit of patronage, public or private. No wonder these mediums make natural homes for outsiders, interlopers, and all those of unsanctioned origins. These are the artists, of course, behind so many of history's watershed works.

Arts that cannot be engaged in cheaply—theatre, architecture, feature film, installation art, opera—face a different fate. The substance of works in these mediums, the very possibilities of what may be realized within them, are evidently constrained by capital, which, unless the artist is of rare wealth, entails winning the approval of others, whether university- and government-arts programs, private sponsors, or (at one time) the church. This puts clear limits on which visions can be realized, and which artists supported: the pedigreed and socialized. Nothing unfathomable or outré has much chance of seeing the light of day.

Granted, there are projects within these arts for which small budgets suffice, and some are among the greatest exemplars of art simpliciter. Yet one can't but notice, in experiencing these works, the way that economic conditions have disciplined their aesthetic palette, whether it's the sort of film stock and lighting used, or the building materials and locale chosen. And there will always be grander aesthetics that cannot sensibly be reduced in scale and cost without loss. How would one cheaply execute a von Sternberg film or a Gehry building?

Bearing the impress of economics, and therefore of social control, these forms can never be quite as free, as open to radicality, as writing, painting, and music.

Good Fortune

Historical wrongs are often thought to delegitimize later distributions of wealth in a society. If the transfer or exchange of resources in the past was often unjust owing to coercion, theft, imperialism, slavery, and such, how can the distribution of wealth that results, even centuries later, be just? There is something right in this. But the problem of inequality runs deeper.

Suppose a society were to redistribute material resources among its members in an egalitarian manner—the equivalent of starting a poker match with all players allotted the same number of chips. Even if every financial transaction thereafter were voluntary and fully informed, the usual variations in natural aptitudes and economic adventurousness between persons, and simple chance as well, ensures that over time the distribution of wealth will almost certainly not remain equal. Some will rise, and others will fall.

What are we to make of this? Must this be an unjust outcome? No one thinks the last man standing in an unrigged game of poker has transgressed against anyone in collecting the table's money, even if the others have lost all they have. Perhaps, then, there is no *inherent* injustice in inequality, no matter how severe; no upper limit on acceptable riches, no lower bound on poverty, so long as the changes in distribution are achieved by voluntary transactions between equals.

The world is nothing close to ideal, of course, and historical transactions have been far from uniformly just. Yet since there are no clear means of equitable redress, it may be that the best we can do is ensure that exchanges hereafter are as fair as possible. That economic inequality would have emerged even if past transactions *had* been wholly just, though, should help reconcile us to justice's compatibility with even stark inequality, and see that a world of haves and have-nots is unavoidable without the *perpetual* redistribution of wealth.

There is an influential argument for just this kind of redistribution, mounted by Rawls and others, that holds that even unequal distributions based on just transactions may need correcting for, since the uneven dispensation of natural endowments—intelligence, imagination, daring, strength, beauty, and the rest—is *itself* in need of redress. Your raw talents and gifts are not ones for which you can claim moral ownership, since you have done nothing to earn them, the thought runs. So the benefits reaped from them should in some way redound to the collective, through redistribution of various kinds.

Why shouldn't your innate powers be your birthright, though, and not some communal resource the less fortunate are entitled to share in? The luck of the draw, the vagaries of fate—the Greeks thought this was what lent life its drama. A moral stance that has no room for it has lost touch with life as we know it to be.

Editorial, Advertising, Advertorial

It has been fifteen years since the rise of social media and still no journalistic outfit has divined how to recoup or offset the lost advertising revenue, though not for want of trying. At even the most august venues, editors are now expected to attend "audience development" meetings, in which internet metrics are trotted out by twenty-something SEO specialists wearing thick black frames.

One style of marketing promises, or promised, anyway, to save the day: native advertising and sponsored content, where the usual firewall between editorial and advertising departments has been doused. If *this* is what it takes to save the day—marketers directly shaping the stories journalists deliver—one wonders whether the day is worth saving. How the influence of sponsors can fail to contaminate a periodical's editorial spirit, once advertisers begin informing articles, is not easy to see.

Is this an argument for the government's helping to finance the media, as it does the universities? Or indeed, should those universities take the media directly under their wing, where so many of the arts and humanities have long sought shelter?

Perhaps, though, complacency and incompetence will solve the problem for us. The future, after all, promises to bring ever greater amounts of data to bear on the prediction of consumer behavior. In a matter of decades, by making these forecasts far more accurate than they already are, traditional advertising might be so effective—so hyper-targeted—that revenues can be resuscitated. A Pyrrhic victory, yes; but also, it seems, a growing inevitability.

PHILOSOPHIES

Philosophy and Bildung

In my high school years an anthology of European philosophy came into my possession; Spinoza, Leibniz, Hume—early modern thinkers were the focus. Among them, it was Descartes who struck me hardest, especially his *Meditations,* in which—*through* which—he takes apart and reassembles all the world with only his mind's eye. At the time I had no background in philosophy and vague notions of becoming a professional of some sort—a lawyer, a doctor, that sort of thing. But Descartes led me in time to Schopenhauer, and Schopenhauer to Benjamin. Although graduation had yet to arrive, it was already clear the usual careers wouldn't do.

Even now, with a doctorate in the subject long in hand, I find Descartes' philosophical manner, not to say his conclusions, most congenial. Regarding problems as he did —as though you were the very first to do so—puts you at risk, yes, of going over old ground, retracing others' steps. But nothing happens twice. Retracement yields to rebirth; old ideas find new life.

Things are different with twenty-first-century philosophers, who can be grasped only as pebbles on a beach. Coming to grips with a thinker's view requires appraising dozens of alternatives that surround it, in a limitless, low-stakes game of comparison and contrast. In Descartes one finds philosophy practiced with intimacy, proportioned to the scale of a person rather than a community of indefinite scope. A work of philosophy conducted in this mode needn't be hamstrung by footnotes, perpetually bowed before "the literature." Rather, it must earn its keep, if it can at all, through its luminosity; mere fastidiousness—the scholar's saving grace—won't suffice.

Descartes had done his reading, naturally, and was pleased to address the thoughts of his peers; the seven sets of objections and replies to his *Meditations* dialectically engage Hobbes, Arnauld, and Gassendi, among others. But at no point does his work threaten to descend into shoptalk. That is just because his faith lies foremost in the deliberative powers of his own mind, and only secondarily in the thoughts of his interlocutors. Usually dialogue and debate are held to be the engine of philosophical progress. Against this, Descartes explores the epistemic advantages of *withdrawal*, from the jumble of the everyday, the hodge-podge of other minds, and the accidents of history.

Travel and the Good Life

The classical sense of the good life, distilled in Aristotle's notion of *eudemonia,* or human flourishing, seems incongruous with our consumerist dreamscape, which began taking shape at just the time the grand tour emerged as the capstone of an elite European education. Can flourishing, though, really depend on tourism? The idea still lingers from the seventeenth century, though now among all levels of society, as travel has become ever more affordable. Yet are we any better for it? It certainly helps legitimate the march of modernity, industrialization, and the status-hungry middle classes, conveniently justifying all the time and money spent (and earned) on movement that premodern peoples would have regarded as frivolous, a mere luxury of the idle. It is hard, finally, to take seriously that the good life depends upon a culture of superabundance in which recreational travel is possible, particularly when most of history's profound thinkers, whether Kant, Descartes, or Aristotle himself, had little time for gallivanting.

Revelry and Reflection

By some standards, even the examined life might turn out not to be worth living. But that only throws into doubt the adequacy of the standard. A better question: Does reflection really improve a life? That it always does may be implausible, even if Socrates brooked no doubts. Yet can we at least say examination *tends* to improve a life?

A crude populism would encourage us to treat all satisfactions as on a par. The distinctive rewards of a life steeped in self-awareness would then, in principle, anyway, be no greater than any other life, including one that dispensed with reflection altogether in favor of blind revelry in whatever the culture happened to throw up. Yet isn't it critical reflection that, among more rarified goals, helps us sift our pleasures for the richest ones, that leads us toward the more lasting delights of the Macallan over the Famous Grouse or *Raging Bull* over *Rocky*? Even hedonism is best served by the capacities of discernment the life of the mind makes possible.

Past Resistance

Here are a few platitudes about memory. It's subjective. It's plastic. It's often self-servingly selective, when it's not simply fiction. Naturally, autobiography, by which I mean that recounting of a human life in which protagonist and author are one, can't help but inherit these liabilities. They once would have counted as such, anyway. In many quarters—in humanities departments, for some time now, and more recently and troublingly, in American politics and popular culture—acknowledging the frailty of memory and narrative history, whether personal or collective, seems to have brought with it a kind of relief from the age-old demands for objectivity (or even intersubjectivity). In many spheres of life, and especially online, we are now asked to admit to the looseness of memory's grip and the tallness of every tale. It's what authenticity and honesty require, we're told: a frank reckoning with human finitude. But the news isn't all bad (or is it?). For we are also invited to celebrate a newfound power over our pasts, and our presents, too, through a curious form of autonomy that would have come as a surprise to Kant: freedom from the tyranny of fact. Subjectivity, partiality, the fragment, and the shard have all become refuges from the fraught project of assembling wholes.

As a novelist, I have watched closely and with some dismay as this phenomenon has manifested in literary circles. Mainstream critics and readers appear besotted by a shrunken, self-pitying strain of diary fiction. You could call it with some fairness Facebook fiction, to distinguish it from the more formidable versions of the past, like Jacques Roubaud's *The Great Fire of London*, the first book in a notoriously strenuous six-volume cycle of memoirs. Novels by Geoff Dyer, Sheila Heti, Ben Lerner, and Karl Ove Knausgaard, whose own memoir cycle, *My Struggle*, might be usefully compared to Roubaud's, if only to measure the diminution in ambition, seem premised on the notion that if it is our fate to embroider and even fabricate our pasts, insulating our preferred identities from the sharp edges of actuality, we ought to openly acknowledge our fraudulence and fantasize with purpose, even panache. (The White House has taken note.)

For my part, I've never found this particular conscription of the imagination, whether in literature, electoral politics, or daily life, especially appealing. Some liberties aren't worth taking. Reading these authors, one feels that if they had more conviction, they would exercise their imaginations properly in the invention of characters, plots, and settings, without simply lifting them from their own lives; or else they would get down to the painstaking work of research and corroboration that's involved in any plausible (authentic, if you like) history, including autobiography. Instead, they've settled on a middling path, both creatively (why struggle to invent from whole cloth when you can just use your life, your memories to fill in your novel?) and intellectually (why sift and weigh the facts when you can just make up what suits the tale you'd like to tell, the person you'd like to be, whenever reality doesn't oblige?).

The deepest difficulty attending the autobiographical self is one that afflicts art, too: sentimentality. Nostalgia, its most obvious form, is hardly the end of it. For the tint of the glasses needn't be rose. The red of self-lacerating shame or righteous indignation will do just as well, as will the gray of ironic ennui.

Do just as well *for what*, though? Evasion—frequently of oneself. This is what binds the various forms of sentimentality together: the desire to *feel* a certain way about oneself or the world overrides the desire to know the truth about it. Fantasy comes first. Yes, memory is malleable and subject to all sorts of failings, no one can seriously deny this, and no one should want to. But why treat these banal faults as insuperable, a limiting horizon of our humanness? When it comes to personal testimony, we nearly always have some form of corroborating evidence—written records, videotape, artifacts of various sorts, and, of course, *other* people's memories—against which we can check our recollections, supposing we're genuinely interested in the truth.

Now, the *significance* of events may be impossible to settle definitively, no matter how much checking and rechecking we do. But this fault cannot be accounted a failure of memory or narrative; it's simply a consequence of events almost always being able to bear multiple interpretations. That lends no credence to the more extreme claims we now hear, for instance, that all narrative or memoir is really fiction. This claim is of just the same order as the one that all news is really fake, even if the people making these two assertions tend to belong to different political parties.

Rather than any intrinsic limitation on the faculty of memory or the practice of storytelling, it is sentimentality —ginned-up outrage at political goings-on that barely touch our lives, say, or tender melancholia about what America used to be like—that stands in the way of good autobiography, good politics, and good fiction. *That* sounds like something we can work on, though, if not exactly master. Nothing like fate.

About the Author

Mark de Silva is the author of the novel *Square Wave* and the fiction editor of *3:AM Magazine*. He holds degrees in philosophy from Brown (AB) and Cambridge (PhD).

Also by CLASH Books

HEXIS

Charlene Elsby

BURN FORTUNE

Brandi Homan

I'M FROM NOWHERE

Lindsay Lerman

MARGINALIA

Juno Morrow

SILVERFISH

Rone Shavers

ARSENAL SIN DOCUMENTOS

Francesco Levato

COMAVILLE

Kevin Bigley

THE MEN WHO TAKE EYES

Justin Little

CONFESSIONS OF A JILTED JOURNALIST

Justin Little

LAUGHTER OF A SCOUNDREL

Nicholas Goroff

WE PUT THE LIT IN LITERARY

CLASHBOOKS.COM

FOLLOW US

TWITTER

IG

FB

@clashbooks

EMAIL

clashmediabooks@gmail.com

CPSIA information can be obtained
at www.ICGtesting.com
Printed in the USA
LVHW041829231120
672481LV00008B/1977